Michael W. Kirst

From Data to Action

D1051278

HARVARD EDUCATION LETTER
IMPACT SERIES

The *Harvard Education Letter* Impact Series offers an in-depth look at timely topics in education. Individual volumes explore current trends in research, practice, and policy. The series brings many voices into the conversation about issues in contemporary education and considers reforms from the perspective of—and on behalf of—educators in the field.

OTHER BOOKS IN THIS SERIES

I Used to Think . . . And Now I Think . . .
Edited by Richard F. Elmore

Inside School Turnarounds
Laura Pappano

Something in Common
Robert Rothman

From Data to Action

A Community Approach to Improving Youth Outcomes

Edited by
Milbrey McLaughlin
and Rebecca A. London

Harvard Education Press
Cambridge, Massachusetts

HARVARD EDUCATION LETTER
IMPACT SERIES

Copyright © 2013 by the President and Fellows of Harvard College

All rights reserved. No part of this publication may be reproduced or transmitted in any form or by any means, electronic or mechanical, including photocopy, recording, or any information storage and retrieval systems, without permission in writing from the publisher.

Library of Congress Control Number 2012951729

Paperback ISBN 978-1-61250-546-6
Library Edition ISBN 978-1-61250-547-3

Published by Harvard Education Press,
an imprint of the Harvard Education Publishing Group

Harvard Education Press
8 Story Street
Cambridge, MA 02138

Cover Design: Erin FitzPatrick

Cover Photos Getty Images: Thomas Northcut/Lifesize (aerial of street); Ariel Skelley/ Blend Images (children at playground); Pgiam/E+ (school building); Fuse (children running); Medioimages/Photodisc (city street)

The typefaces used in this book are Adobe Garamond Pro and Scala Sans.

CONTENTS

FOREWORD

For decades American teachers have graded Friday spelling tests, unit tests, writing assignments, and end-of-course exams to monitor how their students are learning. These and other forms of data collection are still the norm in many schools. However, advances in technology are providing new opportunities and challenges for understanding how students are doing on their way to preparing for post-secondary education and a career.

From Data to Action: A Community Approach to Improving Youth Outcomes is a timely, compelling, and important book that addresses how school and other community leaders can go even further toward understanding the strengths and needs of their students—by gathering data from agencies across their communities, studying and archiving the information, and using it to improve teaching and learning.

It is a daunting but worthwhile task. During my thirty-two years as a superintendent—in Springfield Township School District in suburban Philadelphia, in Eugene, Oregon, and in Oklahoma City, San Diego, and Boston—it was important for me to reach out to community-based organizations and encourage them to work alongside our schools in support of educators, families, and students in ways that would make a positive difference. Often there were tensions between the community-based organizations and the school district. Funding was frequently the dispute because we were all struggling to increase our resources, and there was rarely enough money to share and allocate them in an equitable way.

At the same time, our sophistication in using data developed slowly over time. In the eighties and nineties, states were required by federal policy to set standards for what students should know and be able to do, and to develop assessments that would show progress toward those standards. Transparency in sharing test results became a clarion call for districts and schools. When the No Child Left Behind Act was passed by Congress, data collection and transparency became even more relevant. The focus on data is certain to continue now that the Common Core State Standards have been endorsed by forty-six states and the District of Columbia, and soon new assessments that are aligned with those standards will be released.

And yet test and other school-based data are, and will always be, only part of the story. This book demonstrates how schools and other agencies that embrace similar goals and interests for young people can work together to focus on academic as well as physical, social, and emotional health issues to advance student outcomes while eliminating duplication of effort. Now is a perfect time for the multiple organizations that serve youth in communities throughout the United States to embrace and use the core knowledge presented in this book.

The Youth Data Archive (YDA) at Stanford University is making a positive difference in helping community leaders align their work. It is a cross-agency, integrated longitudinal data system with a variety of players: public institutions, nonprofit community agencies, and other stakeholders. There are three key goals: supporting community partners' efforts to improve youth services and outcomes; improving interagency collaboration; and broadening the field of youth-focused research.

What is unique is their strategy. The YDA researchers not only compile data but also share it among groups with common interests and a commitment to change for the better. This collaboration also results in the development of a "cross-sector lens" that, as described in chapter 1, "enables policy makers and practitioners to see where youth-serving investments are mutually supportive, where they overlap, and where they disappoint."

Partners from the community who contribute the data—not just university researchers—must identify the targets for research using the archive. Another principle is to engage these users by asking them to pose questions, present findings, and generate actionable knowledge. It is important to understand what users want to know and to provide the information they need in order to improve their focus on policies, services, and programs in their communities.

To be successful, there must also be clear expectations about access to data along with transparency about how it is used. Communication is also a major factor in the success of this approach. Periodic reviews of what is working and what needs reworking are important.

The authors of these chapters make it clear that there are challenges and political tasks that will present some impediments. For example: establishing trusting partnerships among researchers, community leaders, and agencies; negotiating the use of data findings; competition among participants; turnover of personnel in agencies and school districts; organizational complexity; hurdles with regulations; differences across agencies; technical issues such as accuracy of data and data matching; and the capacity of those working with the data. The book, however, offers good examples of how to meet these challenges.

Another major challenge for such a university-community effort is how to conduct research that meets the traditional academic standard of quality and still meet the terms of community partners who are interested in what is important to them; in other words, how to make sure that resulting research is "relevant" and "valid" and aligned well with the problems users want to solve, such as how best to improve student achievement on state tests.

As the chapters in this book make clear, it is not easy to integrate data and sustain cross-agency partnerships. However, it is time to understand that traditional approaches and models of collaboration are insufficient. As a superintendent, I regularly reminded the naysayers that data are our friends, and that as educators we need to learn how to use them in fair and transparent ways to improve teaching, learning, and positive outcomes for all students.

From Data to Action provides us with important insights on how to use information relating to young people's lives that is collected throughout the community and across institutional boundaries. Just as importantly, it also shows how much more educators could do with help from others to achieve our common goal of providing the opportunities for all students to graduate from high school ready to continue their education at a higher level, whether at a community college or a four-year college or university.

Thomas W. Payzant
Former Professor of Practice
Harvard Graduate School of Education

1

USING CROSS-AGENCY LONGITUDINAL DATA FOR IMPROVEMENT OF SCHOOLS, PROGRAMS, AND POLICIES FOR YOUTH

Milbrey McLaughlin and Rebecca A. London

A multitude of organizations and agencies serve youth in their communities in different ways. Schools' primary focus is to provide instruction and support for academic learning; human service and health agencies oversee physical, social, and emotional health; law enforcement holds primary responsibility for keeping communities safe and violence-free. Other public and private agencies sponsor out-of-school activities and support youth development in a variety of ways. Despite their common focus on young people, youth-serving institutions typically are disconnected from, and uninformed about, each other's programs, policies, and approaches to serving youth, creating so-called institutional silos. The result can be unintended gaps in the web of support for youth, duplication of services, poorly aligned goals, lack of information about possibilities for resources to be mutually reinforcing, or, worse, missed opportunities to better meet the needs of the community's youth. Understanding how the community as a whole, rather than any one agency or program, meets children's and youths' developmental needs is important for supporting their pathways to productive adulthood.

One way to improve coordination and learning among youth-serving organizations is through data sharing, but this rarely occurs due to practical, technical, or legal difficulties. Each youth-serving organization collects and maintains information on participating youth. For instance, schools collect a wealth of information about students' academic progress, but very little about their social, emotional, or physical development. Afterschool programs collect information about students' attendance and participation in various programs, but are unable to connect this back to their academic learning. Because it is narrowly focused on certain slices of youth service or development, this information does not typically consider the other developmental areas the organization may be influencing or the broader set of community supports and services that shape child and youth outcomes. These are practical, institutional, and conceptual obstacles that speak to the need for a broader perspective, one that frames youth development in terms of the multiple groups, organizations, and institutions that together make up the contexts within and through which young people move from infancy to young adulthood.

In this book, we argue that new cross-sector tools are necessary to support cross-institutional collaboration and that the Youth Data Archive (YDA), a project of the John W. Gardner Center for Youth and Their Communities (JGC) at Stanford University, represents such an approach. The YDA takes a "youth sector" perspective to represent the broad community contexts young people experience and the opportunities and challenges for positive youth development that exist in multiple sectors and institutions. Instead of viewing youth within individual sector-specific contexts such as school or out-of-school programs, the Archive creates a virtual youth sector to provide a comprehensive view of the opportunities and resources available to the community's youth. To support a youth sector, the YDA works with existing community collaborations or provides capacity building for the formation of new collaborations with multiple community stakeholders around a common issue or concern. This cross-sector lens enables policymakers and practitioners to see where youth-serving investments are mutually supportive, where they overlap, and where they disappoint. In this way, the YDA aims to promote community-level responsibility and accountability for youth outcomes broadly considered.

A barrier for researchers, policy makers, and practitioners is how to integrate data to create and sustain cross-agency partnerships across traditional sector confines to support more comprehensive understanding of youths' needs and to offer promising responses to them. Collaboration in the traditional sense—through meetings and other in-person interactions—is a necessary but insufficient first step toward developing the policies and practices that could support youth development across institutional sectors and developmental domains. In this book, we describe how collaboration, capacity building, and data integration across sectors serve to promote youth-sector decision making toward the ultimate goal of improving the long-term outcomes of children and youth.

WHAT IS THE YOUTH DATA ARCHIVE?

The Youth Data Archive is a cross-agency, integrated longitudinal data system containing the data that public institutions and nonprofit community agencies collect on young people who are participating in their programs. The archive is developed through university-community partnerships with researchers at the Gardner Center and participating community agencies and stakeholders. The YDA was launched in 2005 on the premise that community youth development required systems-level change and that cross-agency analyses could enable our partner communities to work across institutional boundaries. Toward this end, the Gardner Center worked closely with specific communities in the San Francisco Bay Area to address these challenges within the local context, building on the strengths and concerns of each community. Initial funding for the YDA came from foundations interested in supporting collaborative approaches to community youth development, and from Stanford University, as part of its larger mission of strengthening university-community relationships.[1] Now that the YDA's value to community partners has been demonstrated, the Archive has moved to a fee-for-service model, though grant support remains critical, especially in building relationships with new communities.

The YDA has grown from work with a single Bay Area community to deep involvement with two Bay Area communities and newer relationships with several more. We are just beginning the first nonlocal YDA in a more distant community. The archive's base is made up of students in public school districts, which range in size from about 9,000 on the smaller end to 48,000 on the larger end. Partners include school districts, higher education institutions, county education offices, county health organizations, social service and welfare agencies, city agencies such as park and recreation, and multiple community-based organizations. The YDA is not a lookup system, meaning that agencies cannot use the archive to examine individual students across institutions and sectors. Rather it is a research tool intended to help agency leaders ask research questions and view aggregate findings without seeing individual students' outcomes or identities.

The YDA's goals are threefold: to support community partners' efforts to improve youth services and outcomes; to foster interagency collaboration and an ability to see their different services as part of the same system of support for young people; and to contribute to the larger field of youth-focused research. Agencies that participate in the YDA agree to share their individual-level data with each other and the JGC for research purposes in order to ask and answer questions about youth that they otherwise would be unable to examine. The archive holds individual-level data for young people living in several San Francisco Bay Area communities from a variety of public and private agencies, including school districts, postsecondary institutions, county human services agencies, county health departments, city parks and recreation departments, and local or regional nonprofit youth-serving agencies. The data are linked individually across organizations and over time to create a longitudinal record of youths' schooling, their participation in community programs or services, and various developmental outcomes. YDA staff are responsible for all the technical elements of creating the data archive, including negotiating

4

access to the data and identifying protocols for secure, low-burden data transfer, data matching, and analysis.

The Youth Data Archive allows contributing agencies to examine questions that combine information about the children and youth they serve with data from other agencies, often for the first time. YDA analyses enable local policy makers and practitioners to look across institutional boundaries and develop joint responses to shared concerns as well as a cross-agency agenda aimed at improved youth outcomes. YDA analyses have examined questions that focus on a variety of developmental stages and areas. As will be described in the chapters of this book, we have studied key schooling transitions, including from preschool to elementary school and from high school to postsecondary education. We have also examined some of the most vulnerable student populations, studying educational outcomes of young people in foster care and in alternative education settings. We have crossed sectors by examining interactions between academic and health outcomes, as well as health outcomes in the context of afterschool programming. The YDA process has engaged diverse partners in collaborative and iterative processes to define research topics and questions, to conduct and understand analyses, and to use the findings to support ongoing action in the community.

The Youth Data Archive is not the first or only effort to tackle the problem of disconnection and lack of communication among community-level youth-serving agencies. The Kids Integrated Data System (KIDS) in Philadelphia, created by researchers at the University of Pennsylvania, combines data from school districts and various social service agencies into an integrated system with the goal of supporting research, informing program and policy decisions affecting youth, and improving the services available to children and their families.[2] Hartford Connects II helps youth-serving agencies track youth outcomes and improve services for youth through a shared Web-based data management and reporting system, but does not include an external research or university partner.[3] The University of Chicago Consortium on School Research is a capacity-building partnership between the University of Chicago and Chicago public schools to expand communication among researchers, policy makers, and practitioners in support of positive school reform.[4] Some states have also set up formal data systems that link educational data across systems, such as Florida's Education Data Warehouse that contains student data from kindergarten or preschool through graduate school (K–20 or preK–20).[5]

Even with these few examples, cross-agency data sharing through a university-community partnership with a user-driven action-oriented framework continues to be rare.

YDA GUIDING PRINCIPLES

Several features distinguish the Youth Data Archive's relationships with communities and serve as operational foundations for its activities. One is the Gardner Center's stance as a *neutral third party*; the YDA holds data for the benefit of the community as a whole rather than for any particular government or nonprofit agency or advocacy group. The research agenda is driven by partners' identified data or research needs rather than by the university researchers themselves. This feature is important because in order for the findings to be actionable for community partners, they must reflect current policy or practice discussions taking place in the community. The Archive's unique contribution to these discussions is its ability to link across sectors, which is a feature of all YDA analyses.

Community ownership of the data is a second essential YDA principle. One strategy to foster an agency's willingness to join the YDA is the establishment of data use agreements that describe the ways that agencies retain ownership or control of their data. For example, the data use agreements state that data contributors have review and sign-off authority over any published YDA product or presentation. This strategy responds to stakeholders' political concerns that their data, in the hands of another public or private youth-serving group, or in the hands of university researchers, could be used to embarrass them, misrepresent them, or initiate legal action. Many YDA community partners have said that they could not or would not have participated in the YDA without these formalized understandings. Examples of data use agreements are provided in appendixes 2 and 3.

Related to community ownership is a third YDA principle, a *user-focused* approach to posing questions, presenting findings, and generating actionable knowledge. The YDA attends to what users want to know and act on, with the intention of providing information to stakeholders to draw upon in their decision making about youth policy, programs, and services. Key to the user-focused approach and to the overall goals of the Archive is that the analyses be cross-agency (involving two or more contributing partners) and that they be actionable. In line with this approach, the YDA focuses in particular on capacity building among community partners—how to ask researchable questions, how to "read" findings, how to provide data needed to examine pressing questions, how to connect to the broader literature and experience—and on supporting them in moving from research to action. Research products respond to the needs of stakeholders who requested the analysis and provided data to conduct it. Beyond that, products are also often developed with policy makers or the academic field as the primary audience. YDA staff provide analytical expertise and take the lead in producing research reports and briefs. Ultimate responsibility for deriving implications for action, however, sits with the Archive's community partners. Because partners identify the research questions or topics, the YDA responds more to community needs than to the academic field and therefore operates according to users' conceptions of research reliability and validity as well as the utility of data analyses.

A fourth YDA operating principle is that of researchers' *long-term commitment* to community partners. This stance influences both the YDA's approach to analysis and the nature of the researchers' involvement. The relationships built with YDA and JGC personnel have been critical to the willingness of community partners to pursue problematic issues of practice and policy. YDA staff take an iterative approach to the research, which promotes capacity building and sharing back at multiple points during an analysis. This strategy serves, on the one hand, to keep the community engaged during what can be a lengthy research process, and on the other, to keep researchers in touch with community needs and focused on how the findings might be most useful as they complete their analyses.

Intentionally, YDA analyses build upon one another as a way for community partners to pose new questions or dig deeper into an area of concern. The long-term commitment and iterative process for each analysis builds trust and communication, encouraging stakeholders to remain invested when analysis takes time. YDA researchers do not depart when a report is completed, but rather continue as participants in conversations about youth policies, partner responses, and promising questions for the Archive to examine. Many YDA and JGC researchers regularly attend community meetings, task force sessions, or advisory boards as a way of staying connected and promoting new collaborations across youth-serving agencies by means of new questions for the YDA.

YDA PROCESS

The Youth Data Archive adopts a design-build-modify stance to research: findings from early analyses spur inquiry into related or different questions, which in turn can begin the process anew. This process suggests a circular schematic, but for the sake of distinguishing partner and YDA (JGC) staff roles, figure 1.1 depicts the YDA process in a more linear format. The steps at the top of the image fall primarily to YDA (JGC) staff, the steps at the bottom to community partners, and those in the middle are done in partnership.

Not shown in figure 1.1 are the initial steps needed to begin YDA discussions, including meeting to understand community partners' questions and discussing the ways the YDA might assist them, providing information about data security and gaining buy-in for initiating the process, completing a data use agreement that allows for data sharing, and, where necessary, securing funds to begin an analysis.

Start-Up Activities

Identify Research Topic The identification of the general research topic and then more specific accompanying research questions can be part of a capacity-building role we play with partners, but it is a shared endeavor. Before data can be transferred for analysis, a general topic of study—for example, the consequences of students' chronic absenteeism—must be agreed

Figure 1.1 The YDA process

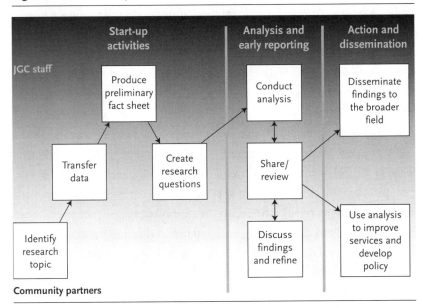

upon and is usually written into the data use agreement. Determining the research focus depends on a number of factors specific to the partners involved, including partners' knowledge of data and research use, the available funding for the work, the developmental phase of YDA staff's relationship with partners, and the nature of policy concerns and decisions that are the focus of the work. The forums in which partners identify the research topic range from informal gatherings to standing meetings of collaborative bodies to meetings of data teams for initiatives. Regardless of venue, YDA researchers encourage partners to identify topics salient to them and to anticipate future decisions which analyses findings might inform.

Data Transfer Data transfer to the Youth Data Archive primarily falls to the management information system or information technology staff at partner agencies. They extract the data based on the elements specified in the data use agreement, put them in a transferable format, and make them ready for in-person pickup by Archive staff (YDA does not accept e-mail data transfers). Archive researchers make every effort to minimize the burden on partners of data extraction and transfer; they allow a broad range of formats for transfer and at times have directly assisted with the extraction process.

YDA analyses rely on individually identifiable data, including name, date of birth, address, and occasionally social security number, in order to link youth records across institutions. Data transfers also include relevant program or service participation and outcomes information for each individual, such as school outcomes (grades, standardized test scores, attendance, behavior, credits accrued); child welfare experiences (case status, placement type, placement location, number of placements over time, reunification attempts, services received); afterschool, recreational, or violence prevention program participation; and dosage, mental health diagnosis, and services received, among others. Storing and analyzing individually identified data by these categories is highly sensitive, and such data are therefore stored on a secure server that is not connected to the Internet (appendix 4 provides details on the YDA's confidentiality procedures). The YDA is required to comply with all relevant laws and regulations for data security, privacy, and confidentiality (appendix 1 provides information on these laws and regulations).

Preliminary Fact Sheet   Once the data are loaded onto the YDA's secure server, researchers spend time to learn and understand data fields and formats. This orientation may involve some communication with partner agency staff or consultation with a data codebook they provide for this purpose. After an initial pass through the data, researchers typically create a "fact sheet"—a brief document, not intended for external dissemination, that represents a first attempt to organize, link, and present the data in a simple form for the purpose of discussion with partners. The conversation provides an opportunity for YDA staff to ascertain that they understand the data and that their preliminary analysis is consistent with partners' understanding of the data.

Create Research Questions   Discussion of the fact sheet frequently results in YDA staff and partners working together to develop more specific research questions that are illuminated from these initial results. This step can involve an in-depth discussion of the needs and standing concerns of partner agencies along with a deliberate attempt to make the questions researchable—meaning answerable with available data. Alternatively, it can be a straightforward process if partners come prepared with clear, researchable questions directly tied to an existing initiative or policy opportunity. Ultimately, the discussion of the fact sheet and selection of research questions act as a launching point for YDA staff to begin the more formal analysis.

Analysis and Early Reporting

In this step YDA staff and partners continue to work collaboratively and iteratively as the staff conduct the quantitative analysis and draft a findings presentation, usually an internal report, for partner review. Once partners have reviewed the draft, the two sides meet together again to carefully review findings, answer questions, consider new questions that arise, and discuss implications and potential actions that partners may take based on the findings. YDA staff may return to the analysis to make amendments or even to investigate a new issue that grew out of the discussion. Ultimately, partners review and vet the document within their organizations and approve it for release. Each analysis is converted into a user-friendly issue brief, which includes greater context about the topic at hand and a substantial implications section, along with a two-page front and back executive summary known as a "snapshot."

Action and Dissemination

The final step in the process involves the dissemination of findings through presentations, Web postings of issue briefs and presentation materials, and other electronic communications. At the request of partners directly involved in the analysis, Archive staff frequently present findings to other relevant stakeholders, such as funders and other community partners who were perhaps not data contributors but may have an interest in the findings. When analyses are relevant to the broader literature, the staff will also present research at academic conferences and publish journal articles as part of YDA's field-informing role with regard to the particular analysis topic and more generally to the value of longitudinal integrated data analyses.

Partners ultimately are responsible for taking action on the analysis findings. Without offering specific recommendations, the implications section of Gardner Center issue briefs are designed to both help guide action and to reflect actions that partners may already have taken based on findings to inform the field more broadly. Community partners have begun to request follow-up YDA analyses to investigate how policies or programmatic changes made as a result of YDA findings have influenced youth behaviors and outcomes.

CHALLENGES TO LAUNCHING AND SUSTAINING THE YDA

The Youth Data Archive has faced and will continue to face multiple impediments in developing community partnerships, obtaining and working with administrative data sets, and sustaining the partnerships over time. We lay these challenges out in this section, and return to them in chapter 9 to synthesize across chapters and discuss the processes we have put in place to overcome them.

One set of obstacles to establishing a partnership with community leaders and agencies is political. The presence and involvement of university researchers often raises concerns within the community about how data and findings will be used, including to whom they will be disseminated. Within the community, competition exists among youth-serving agencies for resources and policy supports and can make data sharing seem a risky proposition.

Organizational issues also test the development and operation of an initiative such as the YDA. Partners' financial or capacity constraints can frustrate collaboration and limit attention to YDA needs and activities. At all levels of the community and across agencies, institutional churn associated with new leadership, retirements, or staff reductions complicates the Archive's operations and can undermine established understandings and commitments. Organizational complexity also creates issues when middle management staff, who have to supply data and act on new arrangements, are uninformed about the YDA's goals and partner agreements.

Regulatory hurdles and other formal constraints on data access pose procedural obstacles. Besides being difficult and time-consuming to navigate, they can and do differ across agencies. Furthermore, state and federal policy contexts limit local actionability both in terms of what stakeholders want to know and what they can do with the knowledge. For instance, school district administrators are highly focused on meeting the performance standards set by the federal No Child Left Behind Act. Their questions and the flexibility they have to act on research findings are both tightly linked to the policy parameters associated with that legislation.

Technical issues present additional challenges. For many if not most participating agencies, administrative data sets contain missing or inaccurate data, a reality that complicates matching data at the level of the individual child or developing a comprehensive picture of youth services and pathways. And the YDA frequently stretches agency capacity to provide data, even when it exists.

A final challenge is funding, which affects many aspects of the work. Agency resources typically are insufficient to allow placing priority on data extraction and transfer to support the Archive. Resources to support research reporting, as well as partnership and capacity building, are similarly limited, which often requires the acquisition of supplemental funds to sustain the YDA process.

GOALS AND ORGANIZATION OF THE BOOK

The goal of this book is to present the Youth Data Archive in action and to show by example the YDA's contribution to community leaders and stakeholders as well as to the youth they serve. We highlight community and university responses to the challenges of establishing and sustaining an initiative such as a YDA as they arise in different community settings and focus on different youth issues. Together, the various chapters illustrate the university-community relationships underlying the partnerships and show how YDA processes and outcomes have served to strengthen or threaten them, but in most cases have led to insights into how to better serve youth.

Chapters 2, 3, and 4 describe the development and consequences of YDA work in three different content arenas. Chapter 2 considers educational transitions and looks at preschool transitions to elementary school, the transition of students enrolled in alternative education settings back into comprehensive high schools, and the transition of high school graduates into the local community college. Chapter 3 presents two health-related analyses focused on the relationship between fitness and academics and between afterschool participation and fitness. In chapter 4, the authors describe the process of undertaking cross-sector analyses—those that involve linking educational data to youth-serving agencies outside the school setting—with YDA research on foster youth and chronic absenteeism.

Chapters 5 and 6 are written from the community partner perspective by our partners in San Francisco and San Mateo counties, detailing the YDA's strengths and challenges from the user point of view. Chapter 5 focuses on the structures and strategies that enabled two institutions—San Francisco Unified School District and the City College of San Francisco—to participate in the YDA, and shows how both institutions responded to the findings. Chapter 6 describes the relationships between the YDA and the Redwood City School District, the Gardner Center's first community partner and a pioneer of the YDA. This chapter details the ups and downs of building trust and confidence in the YDA, along with the action that YDA analyses prompted in community agencies' youth policies and practices.

Early YDA analyses contributed to community deliberation about opportunities and supports for youth, but they also highlighted the limitation of administrative data as resources for decision making. The YDA pointed to patterns, gaps, or areas of concerns, but in some cases it was unable to explain the causes of these observations or the direction for response. Chapter 7 shows how supplementary data can address such questions of how and why. The YDA is committed to producing actionable knowledge, but what comprises "action"? Chapter 8 takes up this complex question and sketches a continuum of response to YDA analyses.

Chapter 9 concludes the book with observations about the contributions of a university-community partnership like the YDA to decision making at youth-serving organizations, the challenges facing a university-community partnership, and the lessons learned about strategies for launching and sustaining a YDA.

We commissioned these chapters specifically to inform policy, practice, and research audiences about the value of conducting cross-sector research with existing data to ultimately improve youth service and outcomes. More than simply a called-for collaboration, the chapters of this book illustrate the value of cross-sector data sharing and analysis to support on-the-ground decision making and action.

Today, more than ever before, policy makers who consider entrenched social problems in education, health, discipline, and juvenile justice are looking to new solutions. A cross-sector strategy that includes data sharing is a relatively low-cost approach to informed decision making that can be employed in a variety of local community contexts that have the will to invest in collaboration and collaborative research.

2

TRANSFERRING KNOWLEDGE

Using Data to Examine Students' Educational Transitions

Oded Gurantz and Monika Sanchez

INTRODUCTION

The educational system requires youth to navigate numerous transitions: from preschool into kindergarten and elementary school, from elementary school to middle school, from middle school to high school, and from high school into postsecondary education. These are common transition points for all students, but many students also have a range of other transitions that complicate their educational pathways. For instance, youth in foster care or in migrant or military families, among others, may experience more frequent transitions between schools.[1,2] Postsecondary students are increasingly following a nonlinear path, "swirling" between multiple two- and four-year institutions.[3] Youth are particularly vulnerable during these transitions, as they adapt to changes in their school structure, neighborhood environment, social networks, and other factors. Research has found that youth at transition points frequently experience a decrease in academic performance or increased likelihood of disengagement from school.[4]

Increased collaboration among educational agencies that populate this pathway from childhood to adulthood could result in strategies that help students and their families better manage these transitions, but most educational institutions have few opportunities to communicate and work with other educational partners. The lack of a shared system of accountability among educational organizations creates little incentive for partnership, further reinforcing a siloed approach. By the same token, benefits to increased communication across institutional boundaries are many. For instance, districts could work together to design systems that identify incoming students who are at risk, to ensure that they receive extra support or are monitored carefully for signs of disengagement or poor academic performance. Improved communication among agencies could also help to ensure that students who exit one system show up at their next intended destination, as in the case of students who are released from alternative schools in order to reenroll in a comprehensive high school. These types of actions—where a school or district sends data to another school in which a student seeks to enroll—is permitted under the Family Educational Rights and Privacy Act (FERPA), but such databased connections across educational settings are rare. The opposite approach—where a school or district sends data to a school in which the student was previously enrolled—is currently limited under FERPA regulations, but sending these data "backward" could give schools and districts feedback on how their students perform after they leave, which in turn might suggest proactive actions that could better prepare students for their next educational setting.

This chapter focuses on educational transitions and the ways in which linking data across institutions can help provide information that promotes better outcomes for youth making those transitions. It discusses three Youth Data Archive (YDA) partnerships that have focused on educational transitions. (See chapter 1 for a description of the YDA and its parent organization, the John W. Gardner Center for Youth and Their Communities at Stanford University, or JGC.) The first example is a study of students enrolled in San Mateo County's court and community day schools and their transition back into comprehensive high schools in one local school district. The second example focuses on students enrolled in Preschool for All (PFA), a state-funded, high-quality preschool program targeted to typically underserved students to support their transition into kindergarten and early elementary grades. The last example examines the partnership between the YDA and the Bridge to Success initiative in San Francisco, a project that brings together the unified school district, the community college district, and other community partners, to improve postsecondary completion among underrepresented youth. The conclusion highlights important findings and lessons from this work.

COURT AND COMMUNITY DAY SCHOOL STUDENTS TRANSITIONING INTO COMPREHENSIVE HIGH SCHOOLS

California's alternative education system includes court and community day schools, which are public schools run by county offices of education. These schools enroll a variety of high-need students, including those who are expelled from their comprehensive high school, referred for attendance or behavior problems, homeless, or on probation or parole.[5] California's data systems have been criticized as being ineffective for monitoring students in alternative education settings, especially as students who transition between schools are generally excluded from accountability data.[6,7] Research has highlighted some of the policy problems affecting these students, especially how they fall into a "no man's land," with no single agency capable of being responsible for their welfare. Court and community day school students might benefit from supportive services during their transition between schools,[8] but there has been little research linking these students to their educational outcomes, especially long-term outcomes such as high school graduation rates or workforce participation, because existing data systems are not set up to track highly mobile students across institutions over time. More data sharing is needed to better understand this highly vulnerable population and factors affecting their secondary school pathways.

Local Context

The Gardner Center analysis of court and community day school students was one of the earliest YDA projects. In order to promote the YDA,

Gardner Center staff used their personal and professional relationships to discuss the initiative with local community leaders. The superintendent of the San Mateo County Office of Education (SMCOE) became interested in participating because the YDA presented the first opportunity for San Mateo County agencies to study the outcomes of court and community day school students as they transitioned between the county and local school districts. The county office of education oversees most of the county's court and community day schools, including ten schools at the time of the analysis: three court schools (the Hillcrest juvenile facility for students awaiting court hearings as well as two separate minimum-security facilities for boys and girls) and seven community day schools serving both expelled and probationary youth. Placements could range from one or two days, usually for students awaiting a hearing at Hillcrest, to a year or more at the other facilities. The other partner in this analysis was Sequoia Union High School District (SUHSD), a district that serves students in grades nine through twelve. The YDA approached the Sequoia Union district to gauge their interest in participating for two reasons: the YDA had worked with the district on a different project prior to the court and community day school analysis, and it had large numbers of students who were sent to or accepted back from court and community day schools.

Court and Community Day School Analysis

YDA researchers worked with the San Mateo County Office of Education and the Sequoia Union district to study the following question: for San Mateo County students who left a court or community day school and returned to the Sequoia Union district, how many successfully completed the school year? This question was relevant because completing the school year begins to satisfy the county's stated goal for court and community day school students to return to less restrictive (i.e., comprehensive) school sites. This information, based on linked data, would be new to both the county, which previously received mostly anecdotal information about the success of their students after exit, and to the district, which had not explicitly tracked the progress of students enrolled in court and community day schools.

The YDA analysis focused on just one of many potentially interesting questions about youth in court and community day schools, and it was selected in large part due to limitations in the data. County data contained specific entry and exit dates from each contact students had with their system, but little other information was consistently collected, such as the types of services and supports the students had received. The district's student information systems included academic and demographic data but tended to delete older information, such as students' entry and exit dates, which would have allowed us to study students who transitioned multiple times in the same academic year. Even though data issues restricted our choice of questions, partners felt that examining the characteristics of students who completed the year after returning to a comprehensive high school would serve as a useful starting point to learn more about this important population of students.

After linking the two data sets, we were able to follow 418 students who returned to the Sequoia Union district from the county's court and community day schools during the 2005–06, 2006–07, and 2007–08 school years. Unsurprisingly, transitioning students looked substantially different from the general district population. They were more likely to be classified as English language learners, have lower socioeconomic status (as measured by parental education and Free and Reduced Price Lunch participation), and have higher rates of diagnosed disabilities, all characteristics frequently associated with worse school outcomes. Almost four out of every five transitioning students was male.

Our analysis found that 59 percent of transitioners finished the school year after enrolling in the district, 17 percent left high school to reenroll in one of the county court and community day schools, and 24 percent were no longer enrolled in either school system at the end of the year (figure 2.1). Students who were no longer enrolled may have entered the workforce, pursued some form of career or technical education, earned a General Educational Development (GED) degree as an alternative to a high school diploma, been incarcerated, or been disconnected from the educational and workforce systems entirely.

Figure 2.1 Enrollment outcomes for transitioner students

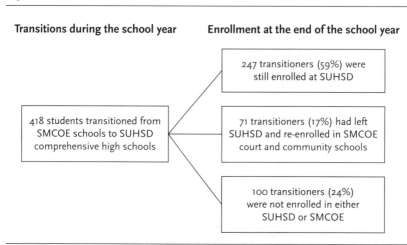

Transitions during the school year **Enrollment at the end of the school year**

247 transitioners (59%) were still enrolled at SUHSD

418 students transitioned from SMCOE schools to SUHSD comprehensive high schools

71 transitioners (17%) had left SUHSD and re-enrolled in SMCOE court and community schools

100 transitioners (24%) were not enrolled in either SUHSD or SMCOE

Though completing the school year is a short-term outcome, we found that it served as a strong initial predictor of students' long-term enrollment. Approximately 44 percent of transitioners who finished their initial school year in high school were still enrolled the subsequent June, whereas just 16 percent of transitioners who did not finish the school year managed to return to the Sequoia Union district and stay enrolled through the subsequent school year. Due to the small number of students examined, we were not able to assess students' long-term outcomes, such as high school graduation rates, but even short-term academic measures produced sobering results. Court and community day school students were rarely able to score proficient on either the math or the English language arts California Standards Test (CST) and were half as likely as other high school students to pass the California High School Exit Exam on their first attempt. Only one-third of transitioners who finished the school year had sufficient credits to be considered on pace to graduate.

The analysis also helped identify the characteristics of students who were more or less likely to complete the year after transitioning into the Sequoia Union district. These included:

- *Placement type.* Students placed in juvenile hall were less likely to complete the year than students who only attended community day schools or students enrolled in court schools. This result was surprising to local practitioners, as students placed in the more restrictive boys and girls court school facilities are generally thought of as those with the highest need.
- *English language learner status.* English language learners (ELLs) were less likely to finish the year in the Sequoia Union district than non-ELL transitioners.
- *Grade level.* Among non-ELLs, transitioners in the upper grades were more likely to finish the year than students in ninth grade. This result was opposite of the "normal" pattern of district attendance, where students in higher grade levels were less likely to finish the year.
- *Academic and discipline background.* Having better high school attendance and completing more credits prior to enrolling in a court or community day school were the strongest predictors of finishing the year in the Sequoia Union district.

Court and Community Day School Actions

San Mateo County and Sequoia Union district leadership identified the Community Day School Advisory Group (CSAG) as the best audience for the analysis findings. The advisory group is a monthly meeting hosted by the county office of education, bringing together representatives from the county, multiple school districts, the county probation department, and community-based organizations, to discuss ideas that could improve the coordination of services for court and community day school students. Advisory group partners proposed a number of specific actions to support these students. Each of the proposed changes was discussed at the group meetings, but partners also discussed some form of these actions even before the YDA analysis took place. Nonetheless, the changes highlight how data, even if imperfect, can provoke conversations on a wide range of topics, and how action can be facilitated by community partners focused on a specific issue. Actions included:

- *Support services for transferring students.* Advisory group partners wanted to identify what services were most effective in helping students succeed, but data on support services were generally unavailable. In the process of having these discussions, the group saw that there was little consistent support for returning students. Comprehensive high schools frequently did not know a student was returning until he or she arrived, and in some cases did not know that a student was enrolled in a court or community day school until after he or she returned. The Cleo Eulau Center, a local community-based organization and CSAG participant, initiated a program with one Sequoia Union district high school that attempted to smooth the transition for returning students by facilitating communication between county and district staff and providing information and counseling to parents and students before and after students transitioned.

- *Course credits.* Conversations about course credit accumulation at the court and community day schools identified two challenges: first, students entering the Sequoia Union district (or other local districts) frequently did not return with their court or community day school transcripts, confounding efforts to place them appropriately; and second, course credits at county schools could be as low as one or two units, which did not align with most districts' policies that tended to assign five units to a particular course. Advisory group members spent considerable time working to resolve these issues so that local districts would be advised of student return, course transcripts would be faxed ahead of time, and transcripts would have course codes and credits that better aligned with those at the comprehensive high schools.

- *Timing of student transfer.* Advisory group participants thought that there might be academic and social issues for students who transitioned in the middle, as opposed to the beginning, of the semester. Our analyses showed that mid-semester transitions were more frequent than anticipated by advisory group participants, but data were not strong enough to draw robust conclusions about the

24

effects of mid-semester transfers on student outcomes. The county office of education has made an effort to shift student transfer to the beginning of the fall and spring semesters.

This analysis provided San Mateo County agencies their first quantitative examination of student outcomes for transitioning court and community day school youth. With more data collection we could have examined students' long-term academic and workforce trajectories, and deepened our understanding of whether particular interventions or school contexts were associated with improved outcomes. This analysis would have required significant resources, unavailable at the time, devoted toward securing data-sharing agreements from the juvenile probation department, local community colleges, workforce training programs, and additional large San Mateo County school districts, as well as repeating the analysis after a period of one or more years. However, the analysis highlights that even linking data from a small set of local agencies spurred conversation that helped create better practices for court and community day school youth.

ELEMENTARY SCHOOL OUTCOMES OF PRESCHOOL FOR ALL PARTICIPANTS

There is widespread agreement that high-quality preschool programs can improve children's educational and social outcomes, particularly for low-income and minority students.[9] The earliest and most influential studies demonstrating the benefits of preschool were conducted on small, high-quality, private preschool programs, such as the HighScope Perry Preschool Program (originally the Perry Preschool Project), the Carolina Abecedarian Project, and the Chicago Child-Parent Center Program. These studies reported that the benefits for students in these types of programs can be seen not only in school, but onward into adulthood. Less evidence exists to show the effects of publicly funded federal or state-run programs, which typically are targeted to low-income, minority, and at-risk students who may not otherwise have access to high-quality preschool programs. The studies that exist on the federal Head Start program and preschool programs in various states show that participating in public preschool programs has a positive effect on students in the short term in terms of their readiness for kindergarten. Few studies have followed these students into the elementary grades.

For many students, the transition into elementary school is the first time they are involved in an educational setting. It is often not until students enter the classroom that teachers and school staff discover whether a child is ready for kindergarten. Many districts are not aware of whether a student attended preschool or, more generally, of what type of experience a child may have received prior to kindergarten. Similarly, once a child moves on from preschool, his or her preschool providers do not find out how that child fared in kindergarten, and so have little information about how successful their program was in preparing him or her for elementary school. On both sides of this transition, educators are cut off from knowledge that may help them improve experiences for the youngest students. If schools and districts knew each child's preschool experience, and if preschool providers knew how their students fared in elementary school, they could determine which programs successfully prepared children for the elementary classroom and improve on those that did not. They could also learn more specifically about the subject areas in which students were best prepared or those in which they might need additional help, as well as about students' social and emotional readiness for kindergarten, before they step into the classroom.

Commissioning the Study and Forming Questions

Preschool For All was a California state-funded program that aimed to provide high-quality preschool experiences to traditionally underserved students. In San Mateo County, PFA was administered by the San Mateo County Office of Education and funded through First 5 San Mateo County. In 2009, a local research firm studied the kindergarten readiness of PFA participants in San Mateo County as they left preschool and matriculated into a number of local elementary school districts.[10] That study found that PFA participants were not only more ready for kindergarten than their classmates who did not attend preschool, but that they were equally ready for kindergarten as classmates with other preschool experiences. These results prompted San Mateo County Office of Education staff to want to learn more about the educational outcomes of recent students in their PFA program. The staff knew of the YDA through its work on the court and community day schools analysis, and because their data were already in the archive, YDA researchers were able to quickly start on a study of the early elementary outcomes of PFA graduates. As the archive also already contained most of the administrative data from Redwood City School District (RCSD), where many PFA programs were located and where many PFA students attended kindergarten, the analysis was then directed at students who attended PFA and matriculated into the Redwood City district. During initial meetings with the San Mateo County Office of Education, the Redwood City district, and Gardner Center staff, two research questions were formed:

1. How did the performance of PFA participants compare to other Redwood City students on early elementary school outcomes?
2. Which PFA or Redwood City district supports were associated with stronger in-school outcomes for PFA participants?

Exploring the Data

A number of issues arose during the initial data exploration that affected YDA researchers' abilities to fully answer the partners' question about what supports were associated with stronger school outcomes. First, the PFA program was established in 2004 as a five-year demonstration project, but the county office of education determined that the data prior to 2006–07 were not collected reliably enough for analysis purposes. Thus, only data from the remaining 2006–07 through 2008–09 school years could be linked to Redwood City district students who were enrolled during the 2007–08 through 2009–10 school years—the years following the students' participation in PFA. YDA researchers also discovered that there was no information on how often a student attended the PFA program (e.g., half day versus full day or how many days per week), data that would have allowed researchers to examine early elementary outcomes for students by their amount of exposure to the PFA program.

What was possible, though, was to answer a similar question about the amount of PFA exposure, but in a less detailed way. Through conversations with San Mateo County staff and exploring the data, we discovered that a number of students participated in the program for two years. We used this information to investigate whether student outcomes differed depending on the number of years a student participated in the PFA program. This in itself turned out to be a useful analysis that essentially answered the same question of whether the amount of PFA participation mattered, just not at the level that we and partners initially believed would be possible.

Analysis Results

Between 2006–07 and 2008–09, 2,084 children attended PFA programs. Of these, 876 moved directly from PFA to the Redwood City elementary schools as kindergarteners. Of these kindergartners, 497 were old enough to track through first grade and 209 through second grade.

Because PFA was targeted to traditionally underserved students who may not otherwise have access to high-quality preschool programs, we naturally found demographic differences between participants and non-participants: PFA participants were more likely to be Latino, have a parent who did not complete high school, be an English language learner, and participate in the federal Free or Reduced Price Lunch program once they entered kindergarten. Because these demographic differences placed PFA participants at higher risk of academic failure, we used regression analysis to control for these demographic differences and found that PFA participants were performing as well as nonparticipants in listening/speaking, reading, writing, and work study skills (figure 2.2). In math, PFA students' adjusted proficiency rates were higher than their non-PFA classmates; these statistically significant results are shown in bold in the figure. When we examined certain subgroups of participants, we found that in math and work study skills, the PFA program added a statistically significant academic boost in kindergarten to groups typically at risk for academic failure such as English language learners, students whose parents did not complete high school, students receiving a special education service, and Latinos.

Figure 2.2 Kindergarten proficiency rates for PFA participants and non-participants (adjusted)

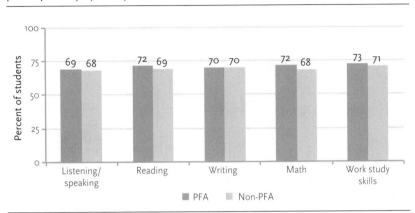

Approximately 17 percent of PFA participants attended the program for two years when they were both three and four years old. In all five academic subject areas, children attending PFA for one year, at age four, had kindergarten proficiency rates that were similar to those of children who did not attend PFA, after controlling for student background characteristics. Children attending PFA for two years, however, had regression-adjusted proficiency rates that were six to ten percentage points higher in many subjects.

The outcomes for students receiving PFA supports were not as clear. PFA offered students and their families a range of support services, including special needs assessment, access to mental health services, learning enrichment opportunities, and parent education classes. In some cases students who received support services—for example, those who received an Individualized Education Plan and families who were referred for mental health services—had significantly lower proficiency rates in kindergarten than other children. Other students whose families participated in parenting workshops had proficiency rates that were equal to or somewhat higher than children whose parents did not participate in those services.

When we followed these same students into first and second grades we did not find a statistically significant difference in rates between PFA and non-PFA students in any academic subject area. This finding likely is due to the smaller number of students we were able to follow into first and second grades because they were not old enough to enter those grades by the time of the analysis. This finding led partners to want to continue to track data to accrue enough students so that a meaningful analysis could be conducted.

Engagement and Action

When Gardner Center staff presented research findings to the San Mateo County Office of Education and Redwood City School District, much of their feedback centered on the differences between student proficiency rates before controlling for student demographic characteristics and the proficiency rates after adjusting for these differences through regression. Though the regression results showed that participation in PFA made a positive difference for traditionally underserved students, partners felt it was important to show that these students' raw scores still lagged behind those of their non-PFA peers. The partners asserted that it was important to report the raw, unadjusted results because this is how students are evaluated in the classroom. With the raw findings, one could conclude that students who went to PFA programs did worse in elementary school than those who did not attend PFA programs. This is technically accurate, but PFA students had background characteristics (such as ethnicity and socioeconomic status) that put them at higher risk of school failure, which is why the program was targeted to them. The regression-adjusted analyses allow for a fairer comparison. Providing raw, unadjusted results is not something that YDA researchers typically include in analysis findings, but we added these figures into the document to ensure that the report matched the partners' needs.

The partners were also interested in standardized test outcomes for PFA students in second grade, the first year in which California students take these tests, but the timing of the report prevented the inclusion of these data. Partners commissioned a second study, which was recently completed, that examined this measure by waiting a year to be able to follow additional students into second grade and one cohort of PFA participants into third grade. In the updated analysis many of the patterns reflected in students' report card outcomes were also found in their standardized test performance. This new study did not include an analysis of outcomes by PFA support service receipt, as the partners knew that these data were inconsistently recorded. They agreed that in any future PFA program, consistent data recording would be important. This type of capacity building of partners was a positive outcome of the YDA process.

The PFA program in San Mateo County is no longer operating, as it was a five-year demonstration project that was not awarded additional funding in light of the state's budget crisis, but the results of this analysis provided fuel for county officials to attempt to revive the program. This YDA work made it clear that any subsequent program will need to do a better job of collecting data to be able to understand the full effects of program participation, particularly the receipt of support services. The findings indicated that longer participation in the program resulted in better academic outcomes for students. PFA partners may encourage this practice in any later iterations of the program.

This analysis provided important information to local policy makers as they considered how to best serve students. It also illustrated the value of examining the outcomes associated with early childhood programs in the local community context. The vast literature on best practices in preschool helped inform the San Mateo County PFA program, but observing the experience of students in their own program and in the early elementary settings into which they progressed would be essential to implementing a program that meets the needs of the provider, the school districts, and most of all, the students.

SAN FRANCISCO'S BRIDGE TO SUCCESS INITIATIVE

More students than ever are enrolling in postsecondary institutions, but completion rates, especially for students in community colleges, remain low.[11] Although many students graduate from high school academically unprepared for college-level coursework, high schools are frequently unaware of these struggles or unable to act on them, as information about their students' postsecondary performance has only recently started to become available. The transition from high school into postsecondary contexts also requires students to develop an educational plan, seek out career or academic counseling to help select the courses necessary to meet those goals, access financial aid, and engage in a variety of other tasks that are not necessarily taught at the secondary school level. Students lacking this knowledge typically struggle to navigate the demands and opportunities of postsecondary settings, and as a result many capable students fail to earn a postsecondary degree.[12]

Both secondary and postsecondary educators have proposed a number of actions to increase the likelihood that students enter college and earn a degree: better alignment of curriculum and placement exams between secondary and postsecondary institutions; shortening the time to degree at postsecondary institutions through more dual-enrollment and college-level work in high school; designing simpler processes to facilitate postsecondary enrollment and access to financial aid; increasing career counseling; and providing more academic and non-academic support services. Accomplishing these activities will require increased dialogue and coordination across institutions, though few resources are explicitly targeted toward facilitating these conversations.

Local Context

San Francisco's Bridge to Success initiative (BtS), funded by an initial planning grant from the Bill and Melinda Gates Foundation, brought together the City and County of San Francisco, the San Francisco Unified School District (SFUSD), the City College of San Francisco (CCSF), and several community organizations to promote postsecondary success for underrepresented students. San Francisco agencies built a strong foundation for this work as they began to collaborate a few years prior to the formation of BtS on a number of initiatives aimed at increasing postsecondary engagement. The BtS initiative also aligned with the goals set forth in a new strategic plan that the school district was developing and with the recommendations resulting from a series of hearings considering the achievement gap evident for the community college's minority students. This initiative provided the first formal opportunity for leadership at the district and the community college to meet regularly and discuss educational experiences for all San Francisco youth, instead of focusing on small numbers of youth connected to specific programs.

BtS partners identified data as a critical component of their work, and the Youth Data Archive was enlisted to provide analytic support to the partnership. They were familiar with the YDA from previous meetings that attempted to identify potential cross-agency research questions. With strong motivation for both partners to engage in this work, along with the YDA's experience in facilitating the legal agreements and data transfer, the formal data-sharing agreements for BtS were signed and data were transferred in just a few weeks. This marked the first time that the school district and City College linked their data on an individual student-by-student level, giving a first glimpse into the educational pathways of San Francisco youth over time.

Initial Bridge to Success Analysis

BtS partners began by focusing on three student "loss points": graduating from high school; enrolling in a postsecondary institution; and completing postsecondary, defined as earning a bachelor's degree, associate degree, or workforce-applicable certificate, or transferring from a two-year to a four-year institution. A fourth loss point—students enrolling in remedial coursework at City College—was later added; students are required to take remedial coursework if their City College placement exams indicate they are not yet ready for college-level English or math.

The YDA linked data from three sources: San Francisco Unified, City College, and the National Student Clearinghouse. The clearinghouse data allow high schools to track the postsecondary enrollment and success of their graduates at most public and private institutions in the United States. The YDA produced a loss point diagram (figure 2.3) that followed a cohort of first-time ninth-grade district students enrolled in the 2000–01 school year. These results showed that 27 percent of first-time ninth-grade district students—1,281 out of the original 4,798—were able to complete their postsecondary education by 2008–09, at an approximate age of 23. The completion rate varied significantly by student ethnicity,

Figure 2.3 Educational attainment of the 2000–01 cohort of first-time ninth-grade students

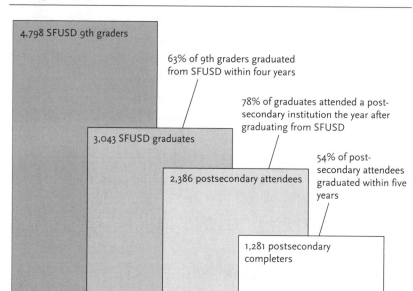

with 48 percent of Chinese students completing compared to just 8 percent of Latino and African American students. The postsecondary completion rate for district students enrolled at City College was significantly lower than the completion rate for students who enrolled in the University of California or California State University systems, driven in part by the high number of students who could not place directly into college-level English or math.

The loss point diagram became the central focus of the BtS work and helped partners identify where attention was most critically needed. These numbers also contradicted some previously held assumptions. For instance, district staff previously believed that almost all graduates attended a postsecondary institution, whereas for the cohort studied, 78 percent actually attended. District staff also thought that most postsecondary attendees graduated from college, and thus were similarly surprised by the low completion rates. These initial findings about student loss points also provided a baseline measurement against which BtS could evaluate progress over time. One promising finding was that the percentages at each of these first two loss points improved since 2000–01; by 2008–09, the four-year graduation rate rose by four percentage points and the postsecondary attendance rate rose by seven percentage points.

Bridge to Success Actions

The first round of analysis was vital to building a level of trust between the district, City College, and the Gardner Center. The district and City College had partnered prior to BtS but had never linked their data on an individual level. Both agencies were initially concerned that YDA researchers would produce analyses that lacked an understanding of the local context, which would influence interpretation of the results. As a result, they spent significant time vetting the initial analysis to ensure that we were interpreting the data correctly. YDA researchers also worked to incorporate a variety of BtS research questions to satisfy the interests of diverse stakeholders within the partnership, but used their own research expertise to help partners identify which questions were feasible and appeared to lend themselves to action. Through collaborating on this initial analysis, the district and City College trusted that Gardner Center analyses would be focused on the questions identified by the BtS collaborative and not on any independent agenda of the YDA researchers, and furthermore, that each agency would have opportunities to provide feedback on results.

This is not to say the first round of analysis was an entirely smooth process. The research needed to occur within real-world BtS timelines that could be as short as three to four weeks, which is significantly shorter than typical research timelines, and required the Gardner Center to invest a significant amount of human resources in the first few months of the initiative. Analysis results were criticized on a few occasions for looking incorrect to BtS partners. For example, the YDA used cohorts of ninth-grade students to examine the relationship between high school GPA and City College placement test results. This cohort analysis produced a much smaller number of high school graduates than what is typically seen in district reports, a number which also included all students who entered the Unified District in tenth grade or later, but YDA researchers felt the cohort analysis was necessary to provide accurate results. In a few cases, partners' criticism was due to inaccuracies in the data extracts or with the researchers' interpretation of the data, and feedback from the collaborative was invaluable to ensure that the analyses were accurate. YDA researchers worked to present data in multiple ways to satisfy stakeholder interests, and efforts were made to resolve data integrity issues as quickly as possible. These challenges highlighted the need to keep partners regularly engaged throughout the analysis process, instead of presenting a set of final summary findings that might contain inaccuracies, be prone to misinterpretation, or arrive too late to be useful to decision makers. We used a small data team, which included a researcher from each organization, to minimize the resources required to vet each analysis, and included additional partners, such as math teachers for all math-department-focused research, as needed.

Even with the impediments described above, district and community college leadership exhibited a willingness to take the main findings and use them to change the way they worked individually and together. We provide two examples of research areas that led to significant policy changes.

Analysis of first-year course-taking patterns   One YDA analysis showed that significant numbers of district graduates who enrolled at City College did not take any core math or English courses their first year, and that these students were significantly less likely to complete their studies at City College even five years later. One previously held assumption among some BtS partners was that students who did not take English or math classes were students who were either academically weak or simply less motivated. However, our analysis showed that this issue occurred for all students, regardless of their previous academic performance in district schools or their placement level at City College. These findings pointed to an institutional problem related to student transitions and, after the district and City College engaged students, counselors, and others in internal discussions, the consensus was that incoming students, who have the lowest City College enrollment status, were being closed out of oversubscribed math and English courses. City College's chancellor used these results to affirm that district students were an important constituency and should be given early enrollment status to ensure that they started City College on the right track. After a first-year pilot showed that district students with early enrollment took significantly more units per semester and were more likely to stay enrolled the following year, this benefit was expanded to all Unified District graduates in the 2010–11 academic year.

Improving English and math placement for SFUSD students YDA research showed that among four-year San Francisco Unified high school graduates who attended the City College of San Francisco, only 26 percent placed into college-level math and a staggeringly low 8 percent placed into college-level English. YDA researchers spent a significant amount of time investigating why so few students were able to begin City College enrolled in college-level coursework. First, many of the district graduates who enrolled at City College did not meet state standards on the English language arts (ELA) or math California Standards Test (CST) in eleventh grade, and these students rarely placed into college-level courses. The analysis also found that 90 percent of students who met state standards in math placed into college-level coursework, but just 24 percent of students who met state standards in English placed into college-level coursework. This English misalignment required partners to discuss a number of issues central to student performance, including the appropriateness of current standards, curriculum, and placement test cutoff scores. Serious, long-term changes are required to address many of the topics discussed above, but BtS partners engaged in some short-term actions, including:

- *Adoption of the Early Assessment Program (EAP).* Most San Francisco Unified high school students take the EAP, a test developed by the California State University system to help eleventh-grade students measure their college readiness in advance of postsecondary math and English placement tests. City College's math and English departments are now accepting a "college-ready" result on the EAP as a mechanism to place students directly into college-level coursework. Based on the historical data, instituting this change in previous years would have provided a small benefit to a few math students who underperformed on the City College placement exam, and would have raised college-level English placement rates of district students by five percentage points.

- *Adjustment of CCSF's retest policy.* The data highlighted that every placement exam, no matter how well designed, will misplace some students. In order to help prevent this from occurring, City College changed the wait time required to retake the placement exam from three months to two weeks, though students are still limited to two examinations per school year. Based on this new policy, 5 percent of entering students chose to retest prior to the 2011–12 school year, and half of these students placed at least one level higher on their English or math exam.

- *Piloting of alternative placement strategies.* YDA analysis determined that high school characteristics, such as GPA, CST scores, and student attendance, predicted which students were more likely to pass their first math or English course at City College. The district and City College began a pilot to allow students who enter the college with strong backgrounds in these three characteristics to start in a math or English course one level higher than determined by their placement exam. This approach is consistent with calls for community colleges to use multiple methods for placement.[13,14]

- *Changing placement exam cut scores.* City College's English department lowered its cut scores (the cutoff levels required to place into college-level English) to better align with the standards set by for the eleventh-grade English CST exam.

As evidenced above, partners were eager to use YDA analyses to understand barriers to student success and engage in actions designed to ameliorate these issues. It would have been impossible to advocate for these changes without research that relied on cross-agency data. District graduates were unable to take core math and English courses due to the design of City College's registration system rather than a lack of student motivation, but without the data it would have been difficult to argue for changes to the registration system. Even though the YDA analysis focused specifically on the pathways of district students, some of the lessons learned, such as the disconnect between the CST English exam and City College's English placement exam, led to changes that will help all students.

This summary of the BtS initiative paints an overly simplistic picture of what was required to make changes to local policies and practices. Many factors contributed to the development of the various policy changes, including: frequent meetings between district and City College staff; various working teams engaged in the research topics, from teachers up to the executive committee that included the district superintendent and the City College chancellor; consistent messaging by BtS partners about the importance of this work; careful attention to the politics of each institution to ensure buy-in; follow-up analyses by the district and community college to ensure that piloted strategies were effective for students; and flexibility on the part of the Gardner Center staff that included altering analyses to reflect partners' specific needs and timelines. More details about these strategies are discussed in chapter 5.

CONCLUSION

This chapter focused on three examples of students' educational transitions: from court and community day schools into comprehensive high schools; from a preschool setting into elementary school; and from high school into community college. The Youth Data Archive was able to provide new and actionable information by linking data across local educational agencies. Partners had not previously linked data as they lacked the capacity to create the necessary data infrastructure and were frequently unaware of the legality of data-sharing initiatives. In the case of San Francisco, where the concept of the YDA was under consideration for some time before data-sharing agreements were signed, partners also needed to identify a concrete, shared goal before they were willing to invest the resources needed to overcome the political or legal roadblocks to data sharing.

Partners who developed their own well-defined research question, as was the case for Preschool for All and Bridge to Success, were more engaged in the research and more likely to act on the findings. Partners in the court and community day school analysis participated because they saw some general benefit to the work, but the research question was developed largely by YDA staff and resulted in fewer changes to local policies and programs. Engaged partners were also more likely to think about and undertake new data collection, as the administrative data used in YDA analyses is generally focused on compliance and may not be well suited to answering "why" students have difficult transitional experiences. During the YDA process, partners discussed intentionally collecting data to help make better decisions, and evaluated the costs and benefits associated with this increased data collection. In the PFA analysis, partners realized that they did not have complete data on parent services accessed during preschool and resolved to collect better data on parent service receipt if the program was renewed in the future.

Partners typically request nuanced analyses, but tend to respond more to the big-picture issues raised by the study findings. For example, although we provided highly detailed analysis in the court and community day school project, partners' key takeaways from the analysis were general: first, finding that even students who completed the school year had poor academic outcomes, and second, that students closer to high school graduation (as measured by grade level or course credits) were more likely to complete. Complex analysis also frequently includes caveats—for example, that the analysis cannot prove causality because of inconsistencies in how data were collected, the low numbers of students in the analysis, or a number of other reasons that can frustrate partners. In the Bridge to Success analysis, the nuanced models could not say definitively that being closed off from core classes was the reason that students were not making timely progress through City College, but knowing this was a common practice emphasized to partners that students' timely transition was an important component to progressing through postsecondary. By connecting decision makers from multiple agencies, local knowledge paired with even relatively simple data can serve as an impetus for people to act.

This chapter describes analyses that involved educational transitions between two agencies, but we know that students are connected to multiple agencies in their daily lives. Youth in alternative education are frequently involved with the juvenile justice system, and the PFA program targeted disadvantaged youth, who may receive additional social services such as public assistance. These other agencies may have services to help support students during these educational transitions, but the effects of these services cannot be captured without accessing these data. In the Bridge to Success analysis, students transitioned from a number of high schools, each with their own set of practices, into different postsecondary systems. Each of these pathways matters and, where the data allow, the analysis should attempt to analyze each of them in order to make the findings more actionable. Researchers can create a more complete picture of students' experiences when they study youth in transition in multiple contexts. The analyses reported in this chapter helped partners see the ways that their data can be combined to generate new and different conclusions; just as importantly, the YDA provided an opportunity for partners from different educational settings to come together and create a sense of shared responsibility around the youth they collectively serve.

3

TYING YOUTH HEALTH AND WELLNESS TO OTHER DEVELOPMENTAL DOMAINS USING LINKED DATA

Rebecca A. London

Health is a key component of child and youth development and an important predictor of young adult and adult health, education, and labor market outcomes. Because health has such cross-discipline ramifications, it is an ideal topic to study with the Youth Data Archive (YDA). Research undertaken with the YDA combines data across agencies with the goal of understanding how communities support positive child and youth development. Health is among the least studied YDA topic areas, in part because it is one of the hardest areas on which to gather reliable and complete data due to both constraints on available information and legal restrictions on sharing identified health data. Still, researchers have conducted two health-focused YDA studies and there is potential for more in the future.

WHY FOCUS ON HEALTH?

Child and youth development covers four broad developmental areas: intellectual, social, emotional, and physical.[1] The field of positive youth development has focused mainly on the first three of these, with far less attention paid to physical development and its role in promoting or hindering development in the other three areas. However, these areas of development are overlapping and mutually reinforcing. Youth health is addressed in many ways in the communities where children live, and it is important to capture these different access points in order to more fully comprehend the role of communities and community agencies in promoting healthy physical development.

Partners involved in the YDA have tremendous interest in health, both on its own and as it relates to their specific areas of focus. For instance, school partners are interested in health as it relates to children's abilities to attend school regularly and in ensuring that children have access to health care services as needed. They are also interested in promoting health outcomes through physical activity at school. Afterschool provider partners, including city agencies and nonprofit organizations, are also interested in health, and in some cases physical outcomes are the main focus of their work (e.g., sports or fitness programs). Both health and social service agencies are also YDA partners, and their focus on child health is a prominent component of their work in providing children with health insurance and other services they need to be healthy.

Despite this broad and deep community focus on child health, creating a cross-agency agenda to study children's health has been challenging. A complicating factor, as is discussed in appendix 1, are the federal regulatory requirements surrounding protection of privacy with regard to health information. The Health Insurance Portability and Accountability Act (HIPAA) lays out guidelines for ensuring patient privacy, but these guidelines also make sharing health data across agencies, even for research purposes, very difficult.

The other main obstacle is lack of available data. Health data are contained in a variety of agency databases, but no single comprehensive database tracks similar information for all children. For instance, the health literature identifies insurance status as an important predictor of whether children and youth access health services[2,3] and is therefore an important factor for understanding child health. However, there is no one source of information for children receiving public health insurance through Medi-Cal and the State Children's Health Insurance Program, and no source that captures information on children who are privately insured or uninsured. A similar challenge occurs for children's access to medical care, their use of services, their short-term and chronic illnesses, and their mental health conditions. Most administrative data on children's health is maintained by their own physician or medical group, and piecing together these data from various sources is nearly impossible.

The most comprehensive data on children and youth come from schools, but most do not presently collect health information. There are exceptions; one district with which we have worked outside of the YDA collects a chronic health survey from all entering students each year, and these data have been helpful in assisting the district to understand absence, targeting of medical services, and other outcomes related to chronic health problems. Schools do maintain information on health conditions that are included in children's health plans or medicine disbursement forms signed by physicians, but these are often not stored electronically. If these data were available electronically, we would be able to use the information to identify students who have chronic health conditions.

In California, critical health information—including mental health— has been collected through the California Healthy Kids Survey (See http://chks.wested.org), which schools and school districts use to track health, school climate, legal and illegal substance use, and other student perceptions and experiences. However, funding for the survey has been reduced, and many districts, including our partner school districts, are no longer able to pay for its collection. Partners in health and education are very concerned about the gaps in information that will result from this.

STUDYING PHYSICAL FITNESS IN SCHOOL AND OUT-OF-SCHOOL CONTEXTS

There is one source of health information that is collected by all schools in California—the Physical Fitness Test (PFT) administered annually to students in grades five, seven, and nine. We have used the YDA to conduct two health-focused projects, both concentrating on students' physical fitness outcomes and how they link to in-school and out-of-school experiences. Unlike the analyses relating to some of the other topic areas discussed in this book, those relating to health were not driven as much by an existing collaborative group focused on that topic. Partners were interested in health outcomes and saw them as important, but, contrary to usual YDA procedures, the specific research questions, and in one case funding for the research, were external to the community. This is in part because we focused on agencies whose main mission is not health-related, but that possessed enough health data to conduct the research.

Both analyses conducted in the health area used data from the California PFT as a proxy for health status. We intentionally decided to focus on physical fitness (a positive) rather than overweight or obesity. The literature on children's health does focus more on overweight and obesity, which are easier to measure and are included more widely in national databases. However, the California PFT includes six components, one of which is a measure of body mass index from which overweight and obesity are determined. Overall fitness level proved to be a better measure in both these analyses than overweight status, but we also conducted most analyses with the obesity measure as well, to align with the literature.

Physical Fitness and Academic Achievement

The question of whether students' physical fitness levels are associated with their academic achievement over time originated in a large partner meeting. At one of the earliest gatherings of YDA partners, we convened representatives from many of the agencies that contributed to the YDA—including school districts, health and social service agencies, parks and recreation departments, and afterschool providers—to discuss the issues they were most concerned about and those they needed to know more about in order to improve their own policy or practice. In this meeting, partners emphasized that health disparities among students—particularly comparisons of Latino to white students—were a major concern not only in the health field but also in education, recreation, afterschool programs, and others. This was the first time health was mentioned by our partners as an important outcome, and it offered a new direction for the work. With just one health measure available to examine, we focused on students' physical fitness testing and worked with participating school districts to obtain these test results from the California Department of Education and link it to students' school records. As this was an early analysis in the life of the YDA, there was no funding provided by partners for the work.

To frame the study, we learned from the literature that for young people, health disparities play out in schooling outcomes. We also learned that most of the research linking obesity (or physical fitness) and academic achievement had been conducted with data from one point in time. This "cross-sectional" data limits the analysis because with just one year of data at a time, it is not possible to determine the direction of the relationship. In other words, if the research points to a significant positive relationship between fitness and student academic achievement, one cannot discern whether the fitness led to improvements in achievement or the converse. There were several longitudinal studies that tracked the same students over time, all using the same national survey—the Early Childhood Longitudinal Study—which is the only national survey that asks both about students' body mass index and their academic outcomes (fitness is not included in the survey). Thus our study using longitudinal administrative data tracking students across physical fitness testing periods from grades five to seven and then across both testing periods and school districts from grades seven to nine made a strong contribution to the literature on this topic.

As shown in figures 3.1 and 3.2, and described in more detail in an article published from the analysis,[4] we found a significant relationship between students' overall fitness levels, as measured by the PFT, and their academic achievement, as measured by the math and English language arts tests of the California Standards Test (CST). CST test scores

Figure 3.1 California Standards Test (CST) score trajectories by overall Physical Fitness Test (PFT) results—5th–7th grade cohort

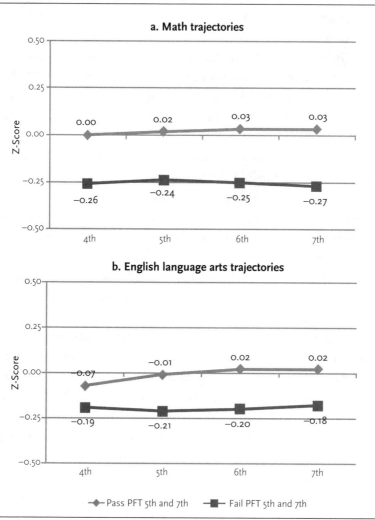

a. Math trajectories

b. English language arts trajectories

are reported as z-scores, which measure the standard deviation from the mean, because raw test results are not comparable across grades or years.

By the time students started fifth grade there was already an academic achievement gap between those who were persistently fit (fit in grades five and seven) and those who were persistently unfit (unfit in grades five and

Figure 3.2 California Standards Test (CST) score trajectories by overall Physical Fitness Test (PFT) results—7th–9th grade cohort

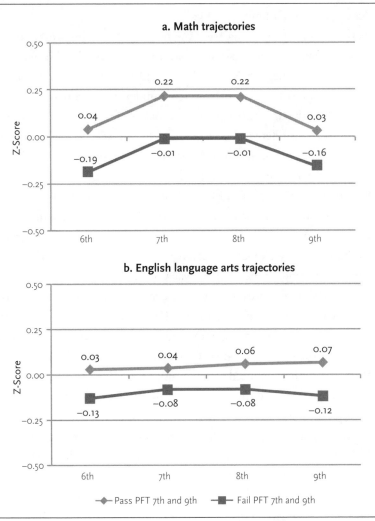

seven). The same relationship held for an older group of students who we followed from grades seven to nine. This achievement gap occurred even after controlling for important characteristics that contributed to both fitness and achievement outcomes, including ethnicity, parents' education levels, students' English proficiency status, Free or Reduced Price Lunch participation, and prior academic achievement. The gap that began as early as fourth grade, and possibly earlier, did not shrink appreciably as students got older and more physically mature.

In the course of reporting back the findings from this work, contributing partners asked us questions about the students who did not fit the mold and were either persistently fit but did not perform well academically, or were persistently unfit and were doing well in school. We continued to analyze the data and learned that socioeconomic status was the key mediator in that students who were unfit but did well in school tended to be socioeconomically more advantaged and those who were fit but did not do well in school were less advantaged socioeconomically.

We presented this analysis in a number of venues, including a smaller task force of partners at the district level who helped to guide the research, as well as at the school board for one district and several conferences and lectures. The work was ultimately published in the *Journal of School Health*. The timing of the analysis was unfortunate, however, as it coincided with the period during which the school districts began to become concerned about their budgets, and adding an emphasis on physical education, or any other type of program, was impossible. However, the superintendent of the elementary district felt strongly about the findings and, we learned months later, used them to support physical activity and fitness in ways that did not require committed funds. The superintendent incorporated physical activity as a strategy to increase student achievement in the district's plan and in the schools' individual site plans, and also used these findings to help obtain a grant from the local health-care district to support more physical education programming at district schools. Because the analysis used educational measures as outcomes, the study was of most interest to school district partners.

Afterschool Participation and Physical Fitness

The second analysis followed indirectly from the first. After the fitness and academics analysis was completed, the Robert Wood Johnson Foundation issued a call for proposals for research focused on Latino childhood obesity through its newly formed *Salud America!* national program office.

Highlighted in the call for proposals was that the research have action-able outcomes and a connection to community that would enable changes to policy or practice based on the results. Our experience with the fitness and academics analysis demonstrated partners' interest in the topic, and this was an opportunity to expand the reach of the analysis outside of the school districts.

Again, the research questions for this study were not initially driven by community partners, but the topic of health disparities and potential solutions was very much in line with partners' broad interests as expressed in the community forum held a year earlier. At the time of this call for proposals, the Gardner Center was beginning to engage in a community youth development initiative that brought together many agencies and organizations that served youth in a variety of ways, including with afterschool programs. And, simultaneously, First Lady Michelle Obama unveiled her Let's Move initiative. We wanted to use this project to help our afterschool program partners think about fitness outcomes and also to align our work within the newly released national frame that called on communities and families to harness their existing resources to make everyday changes that can add up to improved health outcomes for all people, especially children and youth.

Before writing the proposal, we had individual conversations with many of the partners who we hoped would contribute data for the study to gauge their interest in the topic and to get their input in designing the specific research questions that could inform their practice. We landed on a project that assessed the effects of participating in afterschool programs on young people's physical fitness outcomes, again using data from the California Physical Fitness Test that students take in grades five, seven, and nine. The proposal was funded and we were invited to join the *Salud America!* network, which included a total of twenty investigators from a variety of fields all studying different aspects of and solutions to the problem of Latino childhood obesity.

This analysis required gathering data from a variety of afterschool program providers to capture the afterschool experiences of as many students as possible. We focused on the largest providers first, including the

Redwood City Parks and Recreation Department and the local YMCA, both of which ran sports and fitness-focused programs for youth. The Youth Data Archive already included data from two other major after-school providers—the local Boys and Girls Club and also the programs funded at schools sites by California Afterschool Education and Safety (ASES) funds. ASES programs are intended to serve students who need academic support. The ASES guidelines call for providing both academic support and enrichment, which can include a variety of activities, such as arts or physical activity. We also gathered data on high school sports participation for ninth graders, which happens largely after school, and worked with several other smaller organizations to include their information.

The analysis used longitudinal data from the afterschool providers and the California PFT to examine students' participation in afterschool programs over the course of two years along with their physical fitness outcomes and overweight status at the end of those two years.[5] The results pointed to the importance of afterschool program participation in supporting students' ongoing physical fitness. As shown in figure 3.3, fifth- through ninth-grade students who participated in fitness-focused afterschool programs were 10 percent more likely to be physically fit two years later compared to students who did not participate in these after-school programs, after controlling for initial fitness level and other background characteristics. It is important that we control for initial fitness and other characteristics because we also found that students who participated in fitness-focused programs, as opposed to other types of afterschool enrichment, were more likely to be physically fit to begin with. The findings were consistent across subgroups of students, but we found the largest effects of afterschool fitness activities on students who were not Latino, those not receiving Free or Reduced Price Lunch, and especially among those with more consistent participation over two years instead of over just one year. We did not find any effect of participating in other types of afterschool enrichment programs on students' physical fitness outcomes, nor did we find any effects of any type of program participation on students' probability of being overweight.

Figure 3.3 Likelihood of being physically fit after participating in primarily fitness-focused afterschool programs

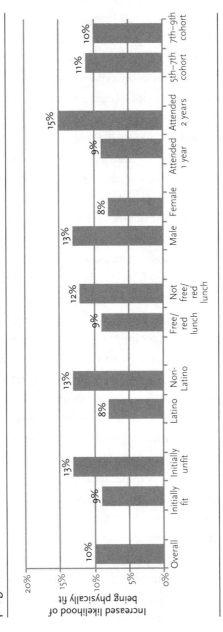

The results were received well by the afterschool program partners, but less so by our school district partners. A major point of contention was the categorization of afterschool programs into those that were focused on fitness and those focused on other types of enrichment activities. Although district representatives did not disagree that our categorizations were correctly assigned based on the criteria we set out, they did not feel that ASES should be categorized as "other enrichment" because, they reported, those programs included a third of students' time for physical activity. Partners' feedback was that the effects of these programs were not adequately captured in the analysis findings and reflected a broader concern that the findings pointed to the inadequacy of ASES programs in promoting physical fitness, a fundamental goal of the local focus of the program. YDA researchers wanted to be responsive to these concerns and, after the initial presentation of findings, went back to the data and reanalyzed it with different categorizations of fitness-focused and other enrichment programs. Even so, there were still no appreciable effects of participating in ASES on students' fitness outcomes. Our compromise with the district was to reword the categorizations and to explicitly discuss their limitations in the issue brief.

A second main area of concern was the sole reliance of the analysis on administrative data, which were unable to explain why fitness-focused programs improved fitness outcomes for participating students. Administrative data were also limiting because they were unable to address the important contribution that schools in the district were also making to student well-being through improvements to nutrition services and a focus on physical activity during the school day, as well as after school. Although this was not the point of the analysis, from the perspective of the school district it was an important omission. We attempted in as many ways as possible to incorporate a discussion of these into our written products and to talk about them when we presented the information. With this attention to their concerns, the school district ultimately signed off on the analysis and allowed us to publish and present the findings.

Although funded externally, this project was discussed at the outset with the Redwood City 2020 Steering Committee, and findings were brought back to this group. We held a meeting of all contributing partners to describe the study and its findings, and we presented twice to the steering committee of the city collaborative focused on promoting positive youth development and outcomes in the city. Beyond that, the study did not receive much dissemination attention at the local level, in part because the school district was not entirely pleased with the research, but also because there was not a naturally occurring group of afterschool partners who were engaged in the discussions of this work as part of the broader context of their operations.

Nonetheless, the study did receive quite a bit of state and national attention due to the *Salud America!* network and our partnership with the California School Boards Association to support dissemination of the findings. The Robert Wood Johnson Foundation and *Salud America!* organized three annual conferences at which plans and ultimately results were presented; attendees included other investigators and a national advisory board made up of leaders in the field of childhood obesity. The California School Boards Association promoted the findings through a webinar and highlights in two of their statewide publications. Findings were also presented at the Best of Out of School Time (BOOST) annual conference and in a public lecture at the University of Chicago. An article resulting from this work has been suggested for inclusion in a *Salud America!* special issue of *American Journal of Preventive Medicine*.

LESSONS AND CONSIDERATIONS

These studies demonstrate the ways that developmental areas overlap and the importance of studying them together in order to capture a fuller picture of youth development. An appreciation for the ways that developmental areas influence one another has the potential to bring agencies together for collaboration; in the case of these two analyses, a cross-agency community collaborative already existed and lent interest and approval. From our experiences conducting and reporting back these health-related analyses, we learned some important lessons about the YDA's potential for continuing research in the health arena.

As with other topic areas, health-related questions must stem from pressing needs among partners for information that will assist them in policy making or program design. Because health is addressed in so many locations—in doctor's offices and hospitals, at home and school, through county agencies and large for-profit insurance companies—there must be a consolidated basis to the research agenda upon which stakeholders agree. Having a commitment from even a small group of stakeholders would also allow for more comprehensive data collection and analysis than is currently available. In both the analyses described here, there was not a meaningful commitment from a group of stakeholders whereby the information to be analyzed and shared back was an important part of an existing planning process. The afterschool analysis in particular was informed by and responded to questions from afterschool partners, but the focus was driven by the Robert Wood Johnson Foundation as the external funder, rather than by pressing questions from within the community. Because these analyses focused on health, one strategy for increasing engagement might have been to work more closely with the health department, but because the data were not collected by the health department, we were unable to garner the attention of policy leaders for this work.

Still, it is clear that health is on the minds of community leaders. In Redwood City there are currently two initiatives in the school district that focus on health needs. In the elementary district, the collaborative has worked closely with the district to implement a community schools model that includes a combination of support services, parent engagement opportunities, and extended learning for students. The support services include a range of options, from transportation vouchers to referrals for counseling or health services. YDA researchers have been active partners in this endeavor through an ongoing research study tracking the effectiveness of community schools in the district (for a discussion of the community school concept, see chapter 6). However, data remain the limiting factor, with physical fitness status continuing to be the only comprehensive health outcome available for study. The community schools address physical health outcomes through referrals, and although we can track whether those referrals occur, we are not able to follow referral recipients to learn whether they obtained services in response to the referral and whether those services were effective in addressing the problem.

The second initiative is at the secondary level, with a teen wellness center that provides health and wellness opportunities for Redwood City high school students. We are working with the district and the high school to focus future analyses on the types of students receiving health and other services at school, their experiences with school environment and climate, and their subsequent academic outcomes.

Perhaps the strongest indication that partners are interested in health-related questions comes from a study requested by the local health-care district to understand the functioning and effects of its newly implemented Healthy Schools Initiative (HSI). HSI is being implemented in four neighboring school districts and is based on the Centers for Disease Control's Coordinated School Health model. In discussions with the health-care district, it became clear that, again, data would limit the potential analyses. Ultimately it was decided that the YDA could not inform the research because the types of data necessary for the research were not available, and that other types of research would inform the analysis.

At the county level, there is a strong interest in health and even obesity, as evidenced by the Get Healthy San Mateo County Taskforce (formerly the Childhood Obesity Taskforce). The mission of Get Healthy San Mateo County (GHSMC) is to work collaboratively with all stakeholders to develop strategies that will reduce and prevent obesity and other health risks of unhealthy eating and lack of physical activity among all children in San Mateo County. YDA team members are involved with the evaluation committee of GHSMC and attend monthly meetings, advise the committee on evaluation techniques, and report on health-related YDA projects. Although a promising place for the generation of health-related topics for the YDA, this group has been focused more on developing programmatic approaches to improve health and is less interested in initiating research projects, though we hope that through our continued involvement, additional health-related YDA analyses may be identified.

Given this interest, it is surprising that more YDA health-related research projects have not resulted. In order for the YDA to continue to focus analyses on youth health and wellness in the future, we would need to obtain new types of health data or data from additional, potentially larger school districts. Some data limitations are insurmountable, but others can be overcome. For instance, one way to emphasize the importance of a health agenda for the YDA is to embed health-related subquestions into our existing YDA projects. These fit naturally into some of the work, including the research we are conducting on student absence (chapter 4) and full-service community schools (chapter 6). Indeed, we have already looked at physical fitness as an outcome in the context of community schools research, but we have not yet been able to link students' health conditions and needs to support service or health service receipt at the community school.

A second way to overcome data challenges is to form new partnerships with organizations that are focused on health as their major outcome and collect data that can be linked to other administrative records to support an analysis. We typically form new partnerships in an organic way, either relying on partners to broker introductions to their colleagues from other agencies or relying on our partnerships with collaborative organizations to form relationships. We are already in partnership with some of the prominent health-promoting organizations in the county, including both the health and human services departments. Representatives from these agencies are part of the community collaborative in Redwood City and are therefore at the table, but these partnerships to date have not resulted in the types of data needed to respond to community health questions. The health department, in particular, has a wealth of data available that coupled with data from more school districts could result in actionable research on the intersection between health needs and schooling. However, to date they have been willing to share only a small proportion of their data holdings with the YDA, which has limited our progress in this area. One source of information the health department shared was publicly funded mental health service receipt among children and youth in the county. We linked these data to school district data, but again, were limited in how to conduct the analysis for two reasons. First, because we could observe only the students who received mental health services through the county—and not those who had mental health problems but received no services or had mental health problems and received services through private providers—we were unable to conduct an analysis of the effectiveness of those services. There was essentially no control group to compare to students receiving services, which made it difficult to tease out the value added of mental health service receipt. Second, there were not enough students in these two districts who received services to conduct a rigorous analysis. Having more county school districts would add to the analysis by providing a larger number of students to examine, which would allow for tracking students over time and potentially more meaningful and robust results in even the absence of a control group.

It may be that to conduct an in-depth health study we would need to collect additional non-administrative data through student or parent surveys (see chapter 7 for a discussion of additional data collections). We would not rule out these possibilities if partners were interested in using different types of data to study youth health with the YDA. Improved data collection procedures could also improve the quality of health data available. For instance, schools do collect health information on student enrollment forms, child health plans, and medicine release forms that are largely kept by individual schools in paper records. If these data were made available electronically, they could be used to study students' health conditions and how they relate to a variety of school-related outcomes, such as test scores, grade retention, and support service receipt.

We will continue to meet partners in the community where they have these conversations and work with them to improve data collection, gather new data, and focus on health as it relates to other important youth developmental areas.

4

"THEY ARE ALL OUR KIDS"

Examining Students Across Sectors

Sebastian Castrechini and Monika Sanchez

INTRODUCTION

Youth are influenced by a multitude of factors beyond the services that any one caseworker, teacher, mental health specialist, police officer, or other youth-serving personnel provides. Youth and their families interact with institutions such as schools or the local human services agencies, community-based organizations providing student programming or parent education, nonprofits, food pantries, health clinics, and a number of other institutions. The combination of services accessed by youth and their families paints a complex picture of a young person's story that no single agency can capture. Because these services span multiple sectors, answering questions about the well-being of youth and families requires research designs that can also cross these boundaries.

Yet there are many barriers to examining youth, especially vulnerable youth, across sectors. Youth who access programs and services across multiple sectors frequently do so because service providers target services to youth with significant risk factors in their lives,[1] which adds to the challenges of collecting data on them. For example, youth in the foster care system are also often part of families that receive public assistance or additional supports like counseling or health services from community-based organizations. Data about these youth who are more likely to experience frequent transitions,[2] and youth who move frequently, such as foster youth[3] and migrant students,[4] often are missing data because records do not follow them when they make transitions.

Furthermore, sharing data across agencies can be difficult. Youth services tend to be disjointed without structures to support collaboration toward common goals. Strong leadership structures that promote cross-sector collaborations are key to making such joint work happen.[5] Also, the agencies that serve youth with risk factors are often stretched to capacity and lack time or resources to devote to improving data collection or collaborating across organizations. Regulations that govern data sharing and confidentiality, described in detail in appendix 1, differ among education, health, and social welfare sectors, further complicating data-sharing arrangements that cross sectors. In this chapter we present case studies of two community-partnered research projects that built on existing collaboratives to illustrate the power of shared data through the Youth Data Archive (YDA). (See chapter 1 for a description of the YDA and its parent organization, the John W. Gardner Center for Youth and Their Communities at Stanford University, or JGC.)

EDUCATIONAL OUTCOMES FOR COURT-DEPENDENT YOUTH

Forming the Research Questions

In the fall of 2008, a group interested in improving educational outcomes for youth in the child welfare system in California's San Mateo County approached the Gardner Center about partnering to address issues associated with this vulnerable population. This group, called the EdSuccess Steering Committee, was convened in August 2008 by Advocates for Children, a nonprofit organization that works with foster youth, and Fostering the Future, a venture fund initiative of the Silicon Valley Community Foundation.

Partners in this group included Advocates for Children, Fostering the Future, the San Mateo County Human Services Agency (HSA), the San Mateo County Community College District, the San Mateo County Office of Education, and San Mateo County Probation Department. The EdSuccess Steering Committee's task was to find strategies to improve the experiences that youth and families involved in the child welfare system have in school.

Recognizing that linked data was an essential piece for informing the initiative and advocating for improvements, the EdSuccess committee formed a subcommittee called the Foster and Delinquent Youth Education Data Working Group. It was specifically charged with exploring options for county stakeholders to track the academic performance of dependent and delinquent youth on an aggregate level and to report these options to the steering committee. The members of this working group identified the challenge of not having reliable, systematic data on educational outcomes for youth in the foster care system. Those who worked with foster youth said that they knew anecdotally that foster youth frequently had difficulties in school, but there was no way to look at disaggregated data on important school indicators like attendance, achievement, discipline, and mobility for these youth. Although educational data are supposed to be captured in the child welfare case management data system, these data are frequently incomplete or inaccurate because records often do not transfer with youth who change placements or schools. The lack of systematic data-sharing practices between schools and social workers further frustrates efforts to look at the experiences and outcomes of foster youth. Similarly, school personnel often do not know which youth are involved in the child welfare system and what types of transitions or in-home placements they may be experiencing—information the committee felt was important to being able to best serve youth in school. One member of the committee likened the scenario to the reporting of disaggregated data mandated by No Child Left Behind and envisioned reporting on achievement for foster youth in the same way that districts must report separately on ethnic and other subgroups. The group felt that having these data would be a critical step in bringing attention and interventions to support foster youth in school.

Some members of the group had worked previously with the YDA and saw the archive as offering an opportunity to link child welfare data to school district data in order to address their concerns. After YDA researchers joined the working group, we jointly identified the following research questions:

- What are the characteristics of court-dependent youth, and how do these characteristics differ by foster care placement types and length of time in dependency?
- What are the educational outcomes for youth in dependency compared to nondependent youth, and how do these outcomes differ by foster care placement types and length of time in dependency?

Some national research has examined similar questions, and California policy makers were also focusing on the issue at the time. Several bills protecting educational rights for foster youth had been passed in the years leading up to the partnership. Still, the group felt that it was important to have local data in order to spur action. Members of the group questioned whether they could rely on studies conducted in other locales because their population differed substantially from the national demographics, with larger concentrations of Latino and Pacific Islander youth. In addition to questioning the applicability of data from other communities to their local context, members emphasized the power of having local data to advocate for policy and programmatic changes with other agencies that serve these same foster youth.

Obtaining Data

Getting data for this analysis was challenging, even with partners who had existing data use agreements with the JGC. A few members of the steering committee took the lead on advocating for working group members to contribute data, speaking strongly from their belief in the importance of the work. Nonetheless, barriers existed. One issue was that people were confused about the how the YDA works; many thought that it was a shared database that partners could use to look up individual youth's records. Some partners, such as the district juvenile judge, wanted this type of individual lookup system, but a lookup system raises concerns about confidentiality that extend beyond YDA protocol in which partners are only able to see each other's data in the aggregate. The especially sensitive nature of foster care data and the vulnerability of the population was a major concern. Staff within HSA's Child Welfare Services department expressed many hesitations about the legality and security of contributing data for the study, even though the director of the HSA had already signed a data use agreement. The issue was finally referred to the county counsel. When a county juvenile judge, who was a member of the EdSuccess Steering Committee, learned of this, she intervened and had the data transferred, offering to go as far as to issue a court order to have the data released. Still, HSA required an amended data use agreement that included specific language from the California Welfare and Institutions Code.

There were similar problems in getting data from new potential partners whose data we hoped to use to supplement the analysis. The working group was interested in learning about outcomes for youth with experiences in the juvenile justice system, but the head of the county probation department was unwilling to share these sensitive data, despite being a member of the group and attending meetings. We were not able to reach an agreement, and probation data were not included in the analysis. Members of the working group had also hoped to engage more school districts in the county (there are a total of twenty-four in San Mateo County), but this proved to be difficult. The group members were strong champions for the educational needs of foster youth, but the time needed by the JGC to get data use agreements and obtain data from additional school districts was prohibitive. Ultimately, we were only able to use data from four existing partner school districts, which was unfortunate because some districts in the county that serve high numbers of court-dependent youth were not included. Still, this was the first time that a YDA analysis included this many school districts in one project.

After receiving all the data, linking them across education and child welfare systems presented another obstacle. The data systems for human services and school districts differ in a number of ways. For example, school data systems are arranged by school year, whereas human services data are organized by service periods. This made it difficult to match school-year outcomes such as achievement scores or annual attendance rates to foster youth experiences that may vary within school years or span multiple school years. Summarizing the data in a way that made sense to partners from both groups required substantial work. We had to condense and then join files that separately contained placement information, address information, and service receipt in order to develop a single case history for each student and then match that to their school records.

In addition to different data structures, a critical part of the analysis was finding common terminologies and concepts for partners who come from different sectors that lack a common language for discussing similar issues or concerns. One of the most challenging issues was finding common ground in the ways that child welfare and school district partners thought about time. School district officials focus on school calendar years (roughly September to June) whereas child welfare officials are accustomed to conceptualizing cases as point-in-time measures of caseload volume and youth placements. Our solution involved making a single annual value for court dependency, placement type, number of placements, and cumulative lifetime as a dependent, to serve as a measure comparable to a school year. This strategy was initially confusing to both sets of partners, who needed to learn about the operations of the other system in order to fully understand and benefit from the analysis. We spent a considerable amount of time in the working group developing a common language and understanding of the research methodology in order to enable partners to comprehend the results and be able to speak about implications.

Analysis Results

Partners were positive about the analysis results, expressing how valuable it was to finally have data on the youth they serve in their communities. Partners said that while they were unsurprised by the results, they also were shocked by the actual numbers attached to the disparity that they had long suspected. One partner said that she cried when she read the report—both because of how bleak the data were and because of how happy she was to finally have the data. As table 4.1 shows, compared to youth

Table 4.1 Educational outcomes for dependent youth compared to non-dependent youth in YDA-partnering districts, 2003–04 to 2007–08

	Dependent youth	Non-dependent youth
Academic test scores		
ELA CST proficiency rate	22%	46%
Math CST proficiency rate	20%	42%
Attendance, mobility, and retention		
Average absence rate	12%	6%
Percent left school mid-year	17%	2%
Percent retained in grade	4%	2%
Progress toward graduation		
ELA CAHSEE (exit exam) pass rate	48%	74%
Math CAHSEE (exit exam) pass rate	50%	75%
Average annual credits earned	40	54
Average annual UC/CSU credits earned	18	33
Discipline		
Percent of students suspended	25%	10%
Percent of students expelled	10%	1%

with no dependency history, dependent youth were about half as likely to score proficient or above on standardized tests, missed school or were retained in grade twice as much, transferred schools mid-year or were expelled ten times as much, and earned about fifteen fewer credits per year. Although these stark findings were not unexpected, findings from disaggregated outcomes by details of youths' dependency experiences were surprising. We learned, for example, that students who had been court dependents for the longest amount of time had the worst outcomes, even compared to other court-dependent students, a finding that partners expected to see. However, students who had recently entered dependency had similarly poor outcomes. Partners reasoned that this could be due to the recency of the trauma of separation or of the abuse or neglect that led to separation; this finding alerted them to the need to pay specific attention to youth in the first six months after entering dependency.

Post-analysis Action

As sobering as these findings were, partners were happy to finally have these data. However, internal discussions of implications brought up challenging questions of potential intervention points. For some these results brought on defensive reactions. In one discussion during a working group meeting when we were discussing foster youth from other counties placed in San Mateo County or vice versa, someone contended that "They are not our kids," to which one convener of the group responded, "They are all our kids." Similarly, a school district employee raised concerns that the poor results reflected badly on the district when they have little control over these outcomes. As these vulnerable youth typically have poor academic outcomes, there was concern about negative publicity unfairly being brought to the school district. At the same time, little accountability exists for foster youths' academic outcomes because they are not normally reported to the California Department of Education as a separate group. These discussions highlighted a fundamental tension about who is accountable for foster youths' outcomes when they cross geographic and agency boundaries.

An important implication that all participants saw was the need for better data sharing across agencies. Although there was agreement in principle, the implementation of ongoing data sharing is a challenge. For example, school district partners discussed adding a field in their data system for identifying foster youth, but there was substantial disagreement on the benefits and drawbacks of teachers knowing this information about the youth they serve, in addition to questions about the feasibility of reliably obtaining this information.

Still, partners were enthusiastic about sharing the analysis results with a variety of audiences. We were invited to present at several meetings convened by the Human Services Agency. One group, called the Children's Collaborative Action Team, is composed of executive directors, program managers, and staff from nonprofit agencies that serve dependent youth and their families. We also presented at the HSA policy meeting, which is attended by Children and Family Services managers and supervisors. This group used the findings to talk about the need to include education representatives on the teams that make decisions on placement changes for dependent youth. We presented to the Foster Parent Association, where foster parents talked about the data as a means to advocate for obtaining educational rights for their foster youth. Additionally, we presented at a workgroup on racial disproportionality in foster youth placements. This group found that having data on those discrepancies and their link to educational outcomes helped them to inform their practice in making placement decisions. For example, the director of Children and Family Services said that the data on disproportional placements into foster homes led him to ask caseworkers to specify the reasons for the placement recommendations they make for each foster youth. We also presented to the Redwood City School District Board of Trustees as well as another school board in San Mateo County that partners wanted to engage in a second round of analysis.

Beyond our presentations, partners and other foster care advocates not involved in the project used the data to advocate for policy and program improvements to advance educational outcomes for foster youth. Our partners from Advocates for Children used the data to advocate at school districts. Through their efforts, they formed a partnership with one school district to pilot a program that provides orientation and support for foster youth making school transitions. Additionally, we learned nearly three years later from the director of Child Welfare Services for the county that he has continued using the data in meetings about foster care placement decisions. He used this example to advocate to other potential YDA partners about the usefulness of the partnership. We also learned of California state legislation aimed at decreasing suspensions and expulsion for foster youth that was influenced by our research. We were invited to present this work at a statewide summit on education for foster youth.

CAUSES AND CONSEQUENCES OF TRUANCY AND CHRONIC ABSENCE

Forming the Research Questions

In 2010, the cabinet members of the Redwood City 2020 (RWC 2020) collaborative went on a retreat to renew and reconsider how they might better serve local youth in the community. One area in which cabinet members thought they might try to expand was data and research. During this discussion the superintendent of Sequoia Union High School District (SUHSD) mentioned his interest in learning about students who are truant and have multiple unexcused absences. The superintendent from Redwood City School District (RCSD), one of the feeder elementary school districts, also expressed concern about students who may have problems attending school on a regular basis for any reason, not just unexcused absences. Students with ongoing attendance issues could be absent for reasons beyond their control, such as a complicated family situation or a chronic health issue, in contrast to students who miss school of their own volition. These complicated factors that place students at risk for missing school further emphasize the need to examine students across sectors to potentially identify any correlations between nonschool factors and school outcomes.

The cabinet turned to the Gardner Center's executive director, who sits on the cabinet, to provide more information on this topic, and JGC staff produced a memo outlining truancy and chronic absence in California, with a special focus on Redwood City. This memo provided information such as California Education Code processes for truancy, a brief review of existing research on truancy and chronic absence, and information on the state's current legislative agenda regarding these two issues. With this document supplying important context, the cabinet funded the JGC to investigate truancy and chronic absence in Redwood City students using the YDA to link students in the elementary and high school districts. The San Mateo County Human Services Agency, San Mateo County Health System, and Redwood City Police Department also wanted to see how chronically absent and truant students interacted with these agencies. The research questions were worded by JGC staff to address the issues generally expressed by the cabinet:

- *The extent of the problem.* How many and what percent of students are chronically absent or truant? What are the demographic characteristics of these students? How has the arc of the problem changed over time?

- *Ways in which this affects students.* What are the causes and consequences of absenteeism in the local area? What demographic characteristics and other factors are correlated with students' absenteeism? What are longitudinal outcomes for students with absenteeism issues? What interventions exist to assist these students?

YDA staff also drafted a detailed work plan that outlined milestone dates for obtaining data from partners, producing interim findings, and sharing the final analysis. The work plan included a clause stating that the timeline would be affected if the data provided by the partners were not received by a specific date. The RWC 2020 partners signed off on the proposed work plan.

Obtaining Data

JGC staff reached out to all of the partners who offered to include their data in the analysis: the school districts, HSA, the County Health System, and the police department. Though the YDA already contained administrative data for both the elementary and high school districts that participate in RWC 2020, these data did not include the detailed attendance information needed for the analysis. They were intended for the districts' normal reporting procedures to the state for Average Daily Attendance (ADA).[6] Soon after the research questions and work plan were in place, JGC staff used their existing relationships with district personnel in charge of data management to request the additional data. However, the workload of district employees did not allow them to deliver these data until several months after the milestone date—nearly consuming the entire analysis timeline outlined in the work plan.

JGC staff also had a prior relationship with HSA regarding their data, though we had not worked together on a project since the foster youth analysis several years before. This new analysis required both parties to go through a different data acquisition process than had been used in previous studies, which led to some confusion and extensive conversations with HSA staff related to the data transfer. Both JGC and HSA staff communicated via e-mail and phone to outline which specific variables would be needed for the analysis. Program information kept by HSA is highly sensitive, and even though HSA had previously agreed to share data for the foster care analysis, we were asking for additional data elements that had not been provided before and for a much broader population than we needed for the foster care analysis, requiring HSA to release sensitive data on children who might not match to the school district data for the analysis. When HSA staff fully comprehended that they would need to provide unique identifiers, such as a child's name and birth date, along with program information to the YDA to link data across systems, they became even more concerned about releasing those data.

Through extensive conversations, JGC and HSA staff agreed to a compromise, to provide the data in two stages: first providing only name and birth date data for all youth served by HSA in its various programs, including foster care and other social services, which we matched to Redwood City students, and then using this matched list to provide program data only for those students. HSA staff who work directly with the data were still unsure as to whether providing this type of data to the YDA was permissible, and they brought a department head into the conversations. The JGC's associate director then also began to participate in discussions. Several months into these exchanges, the two groups had reached a stalemate on releasing the data. Because this was taking place well after the agreed upon milestone dates initially set out by the work plan agreed to by RWC 2020 partners, the JGC's executive director approached the director of HSA about the impasse, who then informed HSA staff that the data transfer could proceed. In this case, it was essential to involve the highest level of leadership to address these extremely sensitive issues.

Data from the County Health System and the Redwood City Police Department were never obtained. After the police department realized that they would need to provide individual level data—as opposed to aggregate figures—they were reluctant to include juvenile justice data in the analysis. Also, while JGC staff began conversations with staff from the Health System about contributing data to the YDA for this analysis, eventually communication from JGC staff went unanswered and the data transfer did not happen. There was also a desire by the cabinet to include data from a second elementary feeder district in a neighboring community. Both school district superintendents on the cabinet approached the second elementary district to encourage the superintendent to participate in the study, but the district did not ultimately agree to be included.

Analysis Results

Though well past the original timeline milestones, we did obtain and incorporate the detailed attendance data from the two school districts serving Redwood City into the YDA. As HSA data had yet to be obtained at that point, JGC staff produced a fact sheet answering the first research question using only school district data: How many and what percent of students are chronically absent or truant? What are the demographic characteristics of these students? How has the arc of the problem changed over time?

In California, students must be absent eighteen full days for any reason to be counted as chronically absent, compared to three thirty-minute unexcused periods for truancy. We found that between the 2006–07 and 2010–11 school years, 4,340 students were truant in the combined districts (RCSD and SUHSD) in any given year. The number of truant students had increased as the student population of the school districts grew over time. At the elementary level, the truancy rate rose from 25 percent to 30 percent during the six-year period. In high school, the truancy rate remained fairly stable during the same time period, though at a much higher rate, fluctuating between 66 percent and 69 percent. Students were much more likely to be absent without a parent's consent in the upper grades, where they were likely to be responsible for getting themselves to school.

Between these same school years, chronic absence rates were steady at RCSD, fluctuating between 7 percent and 9 percent. At the high school level, chronic absence rates were similar (10 percent) during the 2009–10 and 2010–11 school years.[7] In the most recent school year, 950 students in both districts missed at least eighteen full days for both excused and unexcused reasons. It is to be expected that chronic absence rates were significantly lower than truancy rates, as the threshold for being chronically absent is much higher than for truancy. The rest of the analysis focused on chronically absent students, who were missing nearly a month of school and putting themselves at risk for negative outcomes.

In both RCSD and SUHSD, students who were chronically absent were more likely to be in traditionally underserved demographic groups and to have characteristics of students already at risk of academic failure. We also found that chronic absence rates can differ substantially by grade level. During the 2010–11 school year, the highest rates of chronic absence were in kindergarten and twelfth grade (figure 4.1). Fourth, fifth, and sixth graders had half the chronic absence rate of kindergarteners.

After including data from HSA and controlling for student demographics and other background characteristics using regression analysis, we found that the largest statistically significant factor in whether a student was chronically absent was his or her chronic absence status in the prior year. We also found that receiving public assistance did not play a significant part in whether a student was chronically absent, though receiving a child welfare service did play a smaller, statistically significant role for elementary and middle school students.

When investigating the relationship between absence and academic outcomes, also using regression analysis, we found that the number of days absent had a significant negative effect on California Standards Test (CST) percentiles in both math and English language arts (ELA) at the elementary level, even after taking into account students' background characteristics and prior achievement. At the high school level, we found a small but statistically significant negative effect of number of days absent on students' grade point average. For students at both the high school and elementary levels, middle and higher achieving students were at greatest risk of academic decline due to chronic absence.

Engagement and Action

These findings generated iterative feedback from the cabinet that required more analysis. They requested to see the demographic information for chronic absence broken out into more categories. Instead of seeing the characteristics for two groups of students—more than eighteen absences and fewer than eighteen absences—they wanted absence categories for

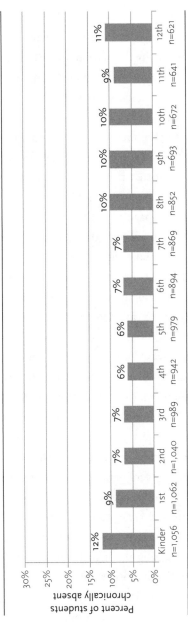

Figure 4.1 Percent of students chronically absent (18+ days) by grade level, 2010–11

students missing 0–5, 6–11, 12–17, and 18 or more days of school. They also expressed a desire to learn where the analysis of absenteeism in Redwood City was situated in the national research picture. JGC staff presented an overview of the research, building important capacity in partners on how to interpret national research and potentially use it in their own local context. The partners were reassured to learn that the results presented by JGC staff, including high rates of chronic absence in kindergarten, have also been seen in other locales and nationally.[8,9] Though answering these additional questions affected the study timeline, it was an essential component in partners' taking ownership of the analysis process and findings.

Another element of capacity building was the use of regression analysis. It was important for partners to understand that many of the other studies they had seen that simply described the landscape of chronic absence did not control for student background characteristics in determining the role of chronic absence in student outcomes. For example, though students who are chronically absent are shown to have lower achievement in later grades than students who were not chronically absent, it is not necessarily the case that absence was the primary contributor, because other factors also influence a student's academic outcomes. It was essential for partners to realize that producing point-in-time counts was not sufficient to understanding the effects of chronic absence, but that by conducting regression analysis we are able to capture how much of the gap is due to chronic absence and how much can be attributed to other factors.

Though the findings were delivered nearly ten months past the initial time frame, after learning these results, the cabinet members were eager to find ways to address chronic absence. They asked JGC staff to inform them about interventions that have been proven to reduce absenteeism so as to use them as a starting point in forming their own strategies for intervening with chronically absent students in Redwood City. JGC staff produced a document outlining what is known about the strategies for reducing absenteeism, the limitations of the current research on the effectiveness of absenteeism interventions, and several examples of successful intervention programs.

Even before the final analysis was presented, the superintendent of the elementary school district began to focus on kindergarten, which had the highest rate of chronic absence, informing parents about the importance of attendance and noting the link between attendance and academic performance. The district also retained the services of a company that provides school districts with various attendance support programs, including attendance tracking, sending letters home to parents about student absenteeism, and identifying at-risk students for early intervention.

LESSONS AND CONSIDERATIONS

Working Through an Existing Cross-sector Collaborative

Ownership of the process   In both of these case studies, a cross-sector collaborative body existed that could take ownership of the process. The foster youth analysis, in particular, was the first in which an existing collaborative group was in charge of the process and we acted in a support role to the existing workgroup. Funding for the project came from a community foundation that was a member of the workgroup, another first for the YDA and an important step in the engagement of the group in the effort. Also, for the truancy and chronic absence analysis, RWC 2020 not only commissioned the study and contributed data but also funded the analysis as a group. This arrangement led partners to steer the study by requesting additional analysis and information and by being actively engaged.

Relevance for obtaining data   Having community agencies advocating for the work was an important factor in getting access to data. For the foster youth analysis, the advocacy of the EdSuccess Steering Committee was vital in our being able to obtain data for the analysis. The steering committee members applied pressure when partners were skeptical about sharing their data, and this activism allowed us to complete the analysis. Similarly, for the analysis of truancy and chronic absenteeism, where there was initial reluctance from HSA staff to provide sensitive data, relationships among members of the collaborative were essential in obtaining a "top-down" communication to staff to release the information. This experience speaks to the essential role of middle management as mediators of the process of obtaining data. The process can become protracted when JGC researchers request data from agency staff who interpret the request as a low priority or outside their authorization. Where there might be a difference in priorities, the upper-level manager must authorize them to act and to prioritize that action.

Relevance for taking action   Having an existing group championing the cause was essential to getting momentum and support for action on the research. The EdSuccess group's commitment to the cause of improving educational outcomes for foster youth was critical to partners taking the findings and using them. They saw the relevance of the analyses that we presented because it was driven by the questions that they had asked, and they were enthusiastic to use the data to advocate for policy and programmatic improvements for foster youth. The partners in the truancy and chronic absence analysis were consistently eager to move forward to develop interventions. They also approached this step as a collective, with non–school district partners involved in shaping action. The elementary school district superintendent stressed that though attendance itself occurs in schools, it would be imperative to collaborate with other agencies to address the issue. She spoke positively about meetings she had already had with the police chief about a mentoring program that he was interested in implementing. It was clear that partners understood that they controlled the process and that implementing effective interventions would need to be championed by the group. In both cases, we learned of actions that partners and other foster youth advocates took on their own (even if, in the case of the foster care analysis, it was not until three years later). This experience speaks to the need to maintain contact with partners both to track these successes and to continue being thought of as partners even after a project formally ends in order to understand the significance of YDA work for policy and practice.

Importance of local level analysis of noted national trends   Even though replicating findings that have already been established may not be appealing to researchers, providing local evidence about national trends can be very powerful for community partners, particularly when the collaborative is a place-based initiative. For partners in the court-dependent youth analysis, having local data was vital to them in advocating for policy and program improvements with local agencies that serve dependent youth. As they said, the results were what they expected, but they needed to have the data to advocate for improvement. For partners in the truancy and chronic absence analysis, knowing from other research that even schools and districts that have high average daily attendance can also have high rates in chronic absence was insufficient to spur action. Seeing their own data illustrate that a considerable number of students were chronically absent and that the highest rate of chronic absence was among kindergartners was eye-opening not only for the school districts but for all of the local partners who may have thought that missing school was not an issue for students in their area. YDA analyses provided the first occasion for partners to examine data on chronic absence across grade levels and over time.

Thinking together about cross-sector solutions   Using cross-sector data to inform cross-sector action is challenging. Cross-sector action necessarily requires creating common language among people doing very different kinds of work in different domains and dealing with different regulations and accountability structures, among other challenges. Having the existing workgroups that already had a mission of thinking about cross-sector solutions facilitated this. In the foster care project, as in many other YDA analyses, partners talked about taking steps to improve data sharing after experiencing the benefits of working together to look at shared data. Still, discussions in the workgroup about the findings sometimes brought up defensiveness over the results. When cross-sector action is involved, it is unclear who is responsible for outcomes and how to hold partners accountable when they all have a role in doing the work that affects those outcomes. As the comment in the foster care case study that "they are not our kids" makes clear, it is important to cultivate ownership of the results by all partners. In the truancy and chronic absence analysis, many of the partners in RWC 2020 were able to see how their agency or organization might contribute to reducing student absenteeism in the classroom, though actions to address these issues are still being formulated. An important contrast between the ways that partners in the two cases reacted to findings may be related to the longevity of the groups, because the EdSuccess group was relatively new whereas RWC 2020 had built an environment of cross-sector collaboration over many years.

Complexity of the Analysis

Making cross-agency analysis relevant to each partner organization   An important reason that partners took action in response to these analyses was the effort by YDA researchers to customize the analysis for each partner. For the foster care analysis, this took the form of tailoring presentations of findings and implications to multiple audiences. Each stakeholder found different implications for their practice, and engaging in these conversations with each audience, especially because partners were often not used to considering data that are not specific to their organization, helped partners make sense of the data. Still, we did struggle to keep the attention of school district partners, who were not as invested in the project as the original members of the workgroup. For the truancy and chronic absence analysis, where the school districts were at the center of the issue, JGC staff provided detailed "profiles" of student demographic characteristics broken down into smaller absence categories at their request. Partners indicated that these additional categories were more helpful to them than a simple "chronically absent" or "not chronically absent" view because they allowed them to see if there were additional ways to differentiate among students with varying levels of school attendance. Though the characteristics of these groups of students were not particularly different from what had already been described with only two categories, knowing this was helpful to partners to be able to speak knowledgeably about student demographics at other absence levels.

Going beyond basic reporting to more rigorous analysis and actionable findings In the truancy and chronic absence analysis, partners had seen studies linking chronic absence with student demographics and academic outcomes.

These studies mostly focused on describing the landscape of chronic absence, conducting point-in-time analyses of disaggregated data to draw a link between student absence and academic outcomes in later years without controlling for other student background characteristics that may contribute to their performance. Partners initially found it challenging to understand why point-in-time and non-regression-adjusted analysis was not sufficient to fully understand chronic absence itself or the role chronic absence plays in student outcomes. Capacity building was essential for partners to understand that using their linked, local data we could examine the predictors of chronic absence in a more nuanced way, illustrating which factors played the largest role in a student's chronic absence status and providing a way for them to better inform interventions they intended to develop. When this analysis took place, state funding for public organizations was diminishing and it was especially important to provide more actionable findings. Regression analysis could determine which of the numerous characteristics that were associated with chronic absence played the largest role—essentially communicating which areas might matter the most.

Balancing complexity of analysis with immediate partner needs and burnout
In both cases, a tension existed between, on our part, wanting to do more complex analyses and, for partners, wanting results quickly. For the foster care analysis, we never got to do the more sophisticated regression analyses because the partners were eager to get some data after having no data for so long and thus did not want to wait the additional time that a more sophisticated regression-adjusted analysis would have required. As with many YDA analyses, there was a risk that the more complex analyses would take more time and that any delay might lose the attention of partners. In the truancy and chronic absence analysis, providing the detailed profiles of student demographic characteristics at the request of the school district partners was done with partners' express knowledge that it would compromise the study timeline. While these additional profiles did not necessarily add anything analytically and did not inform the regression analysis, it was useful for YDA staff to respond to inquiries from partners to build trust and confidence about the analysis. Similarly, YDA

researchers took time to address a request by partners for a presentation to learn where their analysis was situated in the academic research literature, which also impacted the study timeline.

UNANSWERED QUESTIONS AND NEXT STEPS

Because of the difficulties associated with collecting data on youth served by agencies in multiple sectors, our research projects using cross-sector data to understand outcomes for vulnerable youth often illuminate areas in which little previous research has been conducted. Therefore, many questions remain to be examined on these topics. In both analyses, we wanted to understand more about the crossover from additional agencies, such as health services and juvenile justice, but have not been able to due to the unwillingness of these agencies to share sensitive data for a cross-sector analysis. For example, it would be important to understand the extent to which chronically absent students were also receiving publicly available health care to see if medical intervention might curb chronically absent behavior. Similarly, partners on the dependent youth analysis recognized the importance of examining experiences with the juvenile justice system because many dependent youth become delinquents.

Our analyses so far have been limited to determinants and outcomes for specific populations, and we have not yet been able to study interventions to understand factors that can improve outcomes for these populations. As a result of the chronic absence analysis, the elementary school district superintendent implemented several interventions; it would be useful to study these interventions to see if they helped improve student attendance and, if not, to understand ways in which they might be enhanced to do so.

5

"YOU CAN'T POINT FINGERS AT DATA"

Cross-agency Collaboration and Shared
Data from a Community Perspective

Maureen Carew, Laurie Scolari, and Oded Gurantz

RUBY'S STORY

Ruby Dominguez graduated from San Francisco Unified School District
(SFUSD) and decided to get a job in lieu of a postsecondary education.[1]
After working at a minimum wage job for two years, she realized that earning a living wage in San Francisco would be impossible. She decided to visit
City College of San Francisco (CCSF) to "see what this college thing was
all about," with hopes of increasing her earning potential with a college degree in hand. Ruby would be the first in her family or network of friends
to pursue college.

On her first visit to CCSF, Ruby intended to simply enroll in classes.
She expected the process to be stress-free. Instead, she was overwhelmed
by the lengthy enrollment process. As a new first-time student, Ruby had
lowest registration priority and could not get into any of the classes she

needed. Having been away from school for so long, she was not pleased with her placement test score results at CCSF and felt that they did not reflect her potential. She asked for an opportunity to retake the exams, but learned that the college policy required a three-month wait time for retesting; by then she would be well into her first semester. Ruby met with a college counselor who explained that it might be four or more years before she would even be eligible to transfer to a four-year college, due to her low placement scores and the difficulty of accessing the key math and English courses she needed. Her day ended with her in tears, distraught with a sense of being overwhelmed, confused, and alone. Defeated, Ruby decided that college was not meant for her and decided to leave. As she left campus, a small sign caught her attention; Latino Services Network offered a glimmer of hope. As a Latina, she wondered if there were others like her who also struggled with such barriers and wondered if there were ways around them. She wandered into the office and broke down crying. She felt immediate comfort when a counselor convinced her to stay and offered to personally mentor her through the barriers before her.

Unfortunately, Ruby's story is a common one among students who are first in their family to pursue college. Entry into the community college can be a stressful transition that involves social, emotional, and academic adjustments for many prospective students. There are policies that can be especially challenging for traditionally underrepresented students, who typically enter having less familiarity with the college experience. These students tend to have more difficulty navigating the processes needed to succeed in community college, such as developing a plan for graduation and successfully enrolling in the required courses. A recent partnership between SFUSD and CCSF, called Bridge to Success, has been tackling such issues with promising results.

HOW WE SPEAK ABOUT OUR WORK

This chapter focuses on the Bridge to Success (BtS) initiative, a partnership among SFUSD, CCSF, and other San Francisco agencies to improve postsecondary success for underrepresented youth. SFUSD and CCSF came together to make concrete changes to local policies and practices, and many of these proposed changes came from linking data between these two different educational institutions. These linked data provided the first opportunity for these San Francisco agencies to study how students transitioned from high school into their postsecondary education.

This chapter uses the perspective of "we," meaning both SFUSD and CCSF. We make a concerted effort to use "we" and "our" as our common language, regardless of the agency for which we work, because this is how we see ourselves in this work—two organizations acting as one. Too often, agencies work in so-called silos, acting independently instead of through coordinated cross-agency actions, and only seeing students as "theirs" when they are enrolled in their particular system. In contrast, we recognize that "our" actions will make a difference in the lives of the students we collectively serve. In the BtS initiative, even when only one agency was responsible for implementing a particular action, we see this as resulting from our work together, and not one agency acting in isolation. Thus "we" indicates a collaborative spirit between our two agencies; when we want to refer to the actions of one agency alone, we explicitly mention SFUSD, CCSF, or the other agency responsible.

BACKGROUND OF BRIDGE TO SUCCESS

The BtS work formally began in June 2009, when the Mayor's Office worked with SFUSD, an urban K–12 district serving 55,000 students, and CCSF, an urban community college serving 100,000 students, to apply to the Bill and Melinda Gates Foundation for the recently released Communities Learning in Partnership (CLIP) planning grant. This one-year grant provided $250,000 and required partners to work across agencies to identify areas of focus and create a strategy for action.

While the CLIP grant began the formal partnership, both agencies were already engaged in deep conversations and self-reflection around improving postsecondary success for all students. CCSF had begun a series of "equity hearings" to examine the achievement gap between African American and Latino students and their white and Asian counterparts. SFUSD had just adopted a new strategic plan, which also focused on closing the same achievement gap and preparing all students to be successful in college. In addition to collective recognition of these important issues, concrete partnerships had begun to take place. SFUSD formed a partnership called San Francisco Promise with the Mayor's Office and San Francisco State University (SF State) to increase the number of African American and Latino students graduating from SF State. The San Francisco Education Fund secured a grant to partner with three SFUSD high schools to double the number of students who successfully completed their postsecondary education, and the Mayor's Office, SFUSD, and CCSF partnered to successfully launch Gateway to College, a program to reengage and move students who had dropped out of high school toward college completion.

Inherent obstacles exist when multiple government agencies work together, and these projects, which occurred prior to beginning BtS, were no exception. Yet the work progressed, and a great deal of trust was built among these various San Francisco teams while working through the bureaucratic, legal, programmatic, and financial obstacles. We learned many lessons, the most important quite possibly being, *it's worth it!* The CLIP planning grant and the subsequent Gates Foundation three-year implementation grant had perfect timing, giving us an opportunity to focus these different initiatives around a unified framework; but without the shared recognition and desire to improve postsecondary success for underrepresented students, it is unlikely that the money alone would have caused significant action to occur.

CONNECTING WITH THE YOUTH DATA ARCHIVE

Through our early work, even prior to BtS, we recognized the value of data. In 2009 SFUSD began using National Student Clearinghouse (NSC) data to see the number of students who were enrolling in and completing college.[2] It was the first time SFUSD had access to data about the pathways of all students after graduation, rather than relying on students' self-reported information about their plans after high school or returning students' anecdotes that were shared with teachers, counselors, or other staff. Once the data were shared, SFUSD staff were surprised by the number of students not attending or getting through college. These data brought up more questions than answers: Where are the students who did not enroll in college, and do they have some common characteristics? For the students who enrolled in college, where are we losing them, and why?

In order to answer these questions we knew we needed more detailed data, and we enlisted the Youth Data Archive (YDA). (See chapter 1 for a description of the YDA and its parent organization, the John W. Gardner Center for Youth and Their Communities at Stanford University, or JGC.) Our previous projects had not linked data on an individual level, and we saw that the resulting analyses tended to produce simple snapshots of our students that lacked essential details that could have helped our decision making. For example, after the first year of San Francisco Promise, the number of SFUSD graduates who enrolled at SF State increased by 20 percent, but without linked data there was no analysis that described which students were most likely to apply and what could be done to proactively support the next round of students. The YDA approach gave us what we needed, which was individually identifiable, longitudinal data that followed students over time. The leaders of the BtS initiative realized that having the YDA provide data analysis was imperative for us to do the work, especially for stakeholders who required data before they were willing to move into action. Designating 20 percent of the annual Gates Foundation grant funds to data support, which included YDA support and staff time for researchers at both SFUSD and CCSF, also prioritized data-driven decision making and accountability.

YDA researchers had been in conversation with SFUSD and other San Francisco agencies prior to the BtS initiative, but formal data-sharing agreements had not been signed. In the case of SFUSD, the district saw a benefit to participating in the YDA but needed to identify a critical research question linked to their strategic plan before they were willing to commit the time and resources needed to overcome the internal legal and political concerns about sharing data. Once the BtS initiative had formally begun, we were able to champion the idea of data sharing around the specific goal of college readiness, which was a much easier message than the abstract notion of "data sharing." We were also sold on the YDA's approach to community partnerships, which gave us the right to approve publication of their work and not just review their analysis before release.

Having a consistent message of college readiness and knowing that the YDA would use the data to assist our work, instead of simply furthering an independent research agenda, helped us translate this collaboration to internal leadership and negotiate with our colleagues who were initially averse to data sharing. These negotiations were assisted by CCSF's equity hearings and by the changes to SFUSD's strategic plan, described above, that brought a renewed focus on preparing all students for college. Through this process, we finally committed to and negotiated data use agreements with the YDA.

HOW DID DATA HELP MOVE THE WORK?

After we decided to partner around the issue of postsecondary success, how did linking data actually help make change? Using research to make decisions was not a comfortable practice for many in our organizations, and the new research frequently raised questions about the status quo. Dealing with these challenges is hard enough within one organization, and can seem even more daunting when collaborating with external partners, but linking SFUSD and CCSF data helped push people to move beyond the mentality of "this is how it's always been done" and revisit the issue of postsecondary success from a new perspective.

We found that linking data and studying the results served as an impetus for action by highlighting key issues of our practice, providing a neutral forum for partners to discuss the findings, and raising the stakes by bringing more attention to any inequities. We were careful to choose an initial analysis that could be completed quickly and that was less likely to be controversial, as we still needed to take time to build trust among our organizations. We started by looking at the critical "loss points" where we were losing students through the educational pipeline: how many ninth graders graduated from high school, how many graduates attended a postsecondary institution, and how many attendees earned some type of postsecondary credential. These initial data helped build momentum and gave us a neutral set of data points to start discussions about student pathways.

Having these linked data also helped change the way we thought and spoke about our work; instead of "SFUSD" students and "CCSF" students, we began to speak about "OUR" students. This language was used in all our presentations and reports, and helped break down barriers and unify staff around what really mattered—the students we were all trying to help. Working in silos made it easy to blame students' low levels of postsecondary completion on problems within other institutions; CCSF could blame SFUSD for not adequately preparing students for college, and SFUSD could blame CCSF for not knowing how to teach to SFUSD students and not honoring the high school curriculum that SFUSD students had learned. By coming together, we began to appreciate the unique challenges faced by each institution. As a result, SFUSD and CCSF staff initially focused on the parts of their own systems that they could control; this strategy allowed us to gradually build trust, which in turn led to more probing questions and challenging conversations about the problems we experienced with each other's practices.

The linked data brought attention to a number of issues that were previously unrecognized, and that would likely have remained unrecognized had we continued to work in silos. We learned that many SFUSD students were not taking English and math courses in their first year at CCSF, and that these students had significantly lower transfer and degree completion rates even five years later. Using both the YDA's quantitative analysis and consultations with SFUSD students and counselors, we learned that this was occurring because students were locked out of their courses (as in Ruby's case) rather than due to a lack of motivation or academic preparation, as some had suspected. Like Ruby, first-time SFUSD students desperately wanted to take math and English in their first semester but were not accessing them due to a college policy that offered new students the last choice of classes. Using these data, CCSF's chancellor pushed for a change to the registration enrollment system to ensure that all SFUSD students who registered at CCSF the fall after they graduated from high school would receive the courses they needed. This early and powerful action had a huge impact on the partnership. Previous projects had also had opportunities to review data, but the conversations rarely used data to provoke action. For BtS, this decision by the chancellor, subsequently approved as a pilot by the CCSF shared governance system, not only sparked momentum but also created significant buy-in by sending a message to all involved in the project that their voices were heard and would shape how we went about our work as partners. When this policy change was communicated back to the college counselors and other site-level staff they saw the impact of their work and felt empowered, which increased their motivation to participate in the initiative. This response by the chancellor created a major shift in the partnership; at this juncture we officially moved away from finger-pointing and moved toward resolving barriers affecting *our* collective students.

BtS participants were open to learning from these data because YDA researchers acted as a neutral third party with no vested interest in promoting the interests of one organization over the other. YDA researchers were able to present findings that some staff considered negative without being seen as "critical," allowing SFUSD and CCSF staff to approach the research with an open mind. One telling example was CCSF's High School Report, an annually produced document that looked at the performance of students who self-identified as coming from SFUSD. We saw that the basic findings from CCSF's High School Report—the number of SFUSD students attending CCSF in a given year, their placement test results, their long-term completion rates—were not substantially different from the results the YDA produced. Unfortunately, the High School Report had often been ignored by SFUSD staff, many of whom did not completely understand CCSF's placement policies and harbored some mistrust of the findings. For example, the High School Report showed that, on average, 8 to 10 percent of SFUSD graduates placed into college-level English, but SFUSD officials knew that more than half of their eleventh-grade class had met state standards on their annual standardized test (this topic is discussed in more detail below). Without being able to explain this disconnect between CCSF entry-level test score results and SFUSD students' exiting proficiencies, SFUSD staff were inclined to mistrust the entire report as not being accurate. Ignoring this report also allowed high schools to be proud that their students had graduated, until we had data showing some of the deficits in students' performance at CCSF.

We used the data for more than just producing research reports, but also created opportunities for partners to engage in regular discussions about the results and what they meant for practice. SFUSD underutilized the CCSF research report not only because it came from an external source, but also because previously there was no forum where SFUSD staff could come together and react to the data, have a discussion about the findings, or ask CCSF more probing questions to build a shared understanding of the issues. Through BtS we designated forums, such as a monthly steering committee that brought together approximately forty staff from SFUSD, CCSF, and other city agencies, to give staff opportunities to discuss research findings and subsequent actions that needed to occur.

These meetings raised the stakes by bringing more attention to an issue and creating peer pressure for action. One way this occurred was through multiple professional learning communities (PLCs), each of which was focused on a different aspect of the educational system: counseling, teaching, transitions, outreach, and workforce/pathways. Each PLC was made up of faculty from both SFUSD and CCSF, and each group shared highlights of their work at the BtS steering committee meetings. This format made it clear that the responsibility for change was not in any one institution or program but would be shared by the collective group. Sharing their progress at monthly meetings gave each PLC an opportunity to learn from others, but having some PLCs further along than others also added some healthy competition between the groups. This motivated the PLCs to push harder in their own work and design actions to fix the problems they had identified. As another example, SFUSD students constitute only a small part of CCSF, but knowing that San Francisco's Mayor's Office and SFUSD's superintendent were paying attention to the results helped prioritize this population in the eyes of CCSF. When left to themselves, organizations have an easier time deflecting or ignoring negative data. Therefore, promoting transparency and open dialogue was important to create a climate of action among the BtS initiative's participants.

Having forums for discussing research findings, such as the PLCs, gave partners an opportunity to create a unified set of recommendations that captured a multitude of perspectives and experiences. A benefit to this approach was that these recommendations carried more weight than would that of any one individual, especially when the work was grounded in data. A few years before the BtS initiative, one individual at CCSF proposed having a systemic, comprehensive process whereby high school seniors would complete CCSF's five-step registration and placement-testing process during the school day at their high school; this was important, as many high school graduates would not arrive at CCSF until the fall semester, expecting to enroll in courses that had filled up during the fall registration period over the summer. Several individual leaders at SFUSD and CCSF agreed that it was a good idea, but the proposal was presented to district leaders separately, instead of through a powerful partnership, and was not grounded in data that would have demonstrated how transitional barriers are an important issue for equitable student access. However, when BtS advocated for this change it was quickly approved, and the cross-agency forums provided a venue to plan the logistics needed to implement this process. Had this process existed when Ruby was in high school, perhaps she would have completed the appropriate CCSF enrollment steps prior to graduating, providing her with ample time to successfully enroll in CCSF and access the courses she needed.

We used YDA analyses to push for changes, but data are not flawless, and do not necessarily address why students behave the way they do. As a result, we did not wait for perfect data or analysis that would comprehensively answer all our questions. We built momentum slowly by choosing as our first analysis one that could be completed quickly and was less likely to be controversial. To make the findings more meaningful and actionable, we also supplemented YDA's quantitative research with qualitative data from interviews, focus groups, and informal conversations with students and staff. A student advocacy group at CCSF comprised of African American, Latino, and Pacific Islander students that the initiative aimed to serve joined the partnership and contributed with powerful voices. This strategy connected us to how the barriers affected real students. These student voices, such as Ruby's, helped us identify problems of practice and led to concrete changes, such as the early enrollment program for SFUSD graduates. Before making early enrollment a permanent policy, we spent a year piloting the approach with three hundred SFUSD graduates and found that the students averaged a course load of twelve units in their first semester, up from an average of eight units in previous years, and that the increase was mainly due to more students accessing math and English courses. All of these approaches—having both quantitative and qualitative analysis, adding a student voice, piloting and studying changes before full implementation—helped us implement effective policies.

As the initiative progressed, and after we had several small wins, we went beyond the less controversial analyses and moved toward confronting the larger policy issues. For example, one of the more contentious issues was that fewer than 10 percent of SFUSD graduates placed into college-level English at CCSF, with many of these students needing four or more semesters of remediation before reaching college level. Initial conversations touched on very sensitive issues. Was the high remediation rate the fault of the high school district for having graduated unprepared students? Was it the fault of CCSF for having an overly difficult placement exam? Was it the fault of the state for having misaligned curricular standards between secondary and postsecondary institutions? Was it something else entirely? Asking these questions was, at times, threatening to both institutions, as the answers would require some serious rethinking about the way we engaged in our work.

YDA analysis showed that the high English remediation rate for SFUSD graduates was a combination of various issues. YDA researchers determined that the simplest way to present the data was through a scatterplot (figure 5.1). Each dot in the scatterplot represents one student, with his or her eleventh-grade English California Standards Test (CST) results on the x-axis (from zero to 75 questions correct) and the same student's CCSF English placement test results on the y-axis (from zero to 110 questions correct).[3] From this chart we learned three major lessons: 1) The CST and CCSF placement exam were well aligned, as students who scored high on one test tended to score high on the other test; 2) approximately two-thirds of SFUSD graduates who attended CCSF did not meet English state standards in eleventh grade (left box), and these students almost never placed into college-level English (top box); and 3) even students who met state standards (right box) only placed into college-level English (top box) when they exceeded state standards by a very significant amount.

Figure 5.1 Scatterplot of 11th-grade English CST scores and CCSF English placement test scores

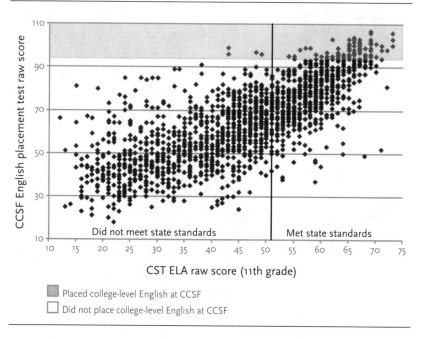

Placed college-level English at CCSF
Did not place college-level English at CCSF

It would have been easy to stay focused on smaller, more manageable tasks, but the ability to learn the answers to these difficult questions helped pull people toward a more concrete understanding of the problem. The English score scatterplot was an effective way of presenting this controversial issue, as it translated a complex topic into a single image. This representation facilitated conversations among staff across institutions and created a common understanding that allowed us to engage in productive dialogue, instead of remaining siloed organizations with negative assumptions about each other's practices. CCSF's chancellor frequently utilized the scatterplot to engage the CCSF faculty in understanding the urgency of the problem, and this diagram helped convince CCSF's English department to lower their placement cutoff scores to more closely align with high school state standards. One lesson for researchers from this experience is that they can help districts and other youth-serving agencies by going beyond traditional presentations, such as regression results, and designing striking visual representations that help organizations better understand the issues they are trying to address.

Our approach to tackling these difficult issues was to work on multiple issues simultaneously, rather than focusing on one small piece of the postsecondary puzzle. One way we accomplished this was through our PLCs, each of which was responsible for addressing different challenges students faced in the educational pipeline. This approach made explicit our belief that there was no silver bullet to support postsecondary success; as a result, individuals doing the work did not feel that their particular department or area of focus was being singled out for criticism—we were in this together. This stance also allowed the more challenging areas of the work, where there were political concerns, data problems, or simply more reticence among staff, to progress at their own pace. Provided that each PLC was making some progress, this approach relieved some of the pressure that might make staff feel pushed into action before they were ready. PLCs that were eager for data helped show more hesitant PLCs that the data were being used to make informed decisions, and not to "shame and blame" anyone for past performance.

As a result of our multipronged approach—using the YDA to analyze linked data, bringing together multiple agencies to discuss the findings, recognizing that each part of the educational system needed to improve, and relying on participants' institutional knowledge to push for change—we developed a number of changes we believe will help students complete their postsecondary education. One was "FRISCO day," which is an all-year, multistep initiative designed to smooth the transition into CCSF. As part of this initiative we brought CCSF's five-step enrollment process into SFUSD's high schools, to systematically enroll all CCSF-bound students as well as those students who wanted to go to college but did not have concrete postsecondary plans. In conjunction with the enrollment process, we designated one day where every graduating high school senior visited one of three local colleges, with CCSF being one of the three destinations. Each college visit was packed with workshops and activities to educate students about what it meant to attend that college and how best to access the multitude of support services. All these steps, which could only occur through a strong partnership between the two organizations, minimized the impediments associated with high-school-to-college transitions that were brought to our attention through both the data and personal stories such as Ruby's. Additional actions from the BtS initiative included a "summer bridge" program to help a concentrated group of underrepresented students get a jump on their postsecondary plans; shortening CCSF's placement test retake policy from three months' wait time to two weeks; and piloting a multiple-method approach to English and math placement to help students begin their postsecondary education in the most appropriate course. This short list does not reflect other work happening in the PLCs that have not yet resulted in permanent changes to the system: facilitating dual-enrollment, implementing early warning indicators, and improving career and technical education, among others.

HOW WE BUILT SUPPORT FOR THE WORK

Although the data supported action, they are only one part of the solution. Changes in policy and practice can take years to implement, but in order to engage students like Ruby we needed to create a sense of urgency, before more students were lost. A number of actions helped us build a strong coalition and advocate for changes. Yet we believe, more than anything, that each organization will have different political and practical challenges, and the work must be attuned to these institutional differences.

First, it was critical to assign leaders who were "champions," either from inside or outside the organizations, who would prioritize the goals of the initiative as a part of their daily workload. We believed that these leaders needed to be middle managers, such as a dean at the community college and an equivalent director at the high school level. The benefit was that middle managers were able to connect to both the highest level of leadership as well as the on-the-ground staff. The connection to high-level leadership was important to ensure that the initiative aligned with an agency's strategic plan and that leadership was prioritizing the work and sharing it as a part of their overall vision. The connection to the site-level staff was needed to establish staff buy-in, lead staff in implementing the changes, and understand how these changes were affecting staff workload. In BtS, these middle managers presented the data findings and the proposed actions to an executive committee that included the chancellor of CCSF, the superintendent of SFUSD, the San Francisco Mayor's Office education advisor, and other leaders. Middle managers often referenced the participation of the executive committee to get buy-in from site-level staff, who were impressed that the top leaders from each institution came together and discussed the specific challenges they faced in implementing the work. Our ability as middle managers to share these findings back with site-level staff and negotiate between the "big ideas" and the "on-the-ground" implementation was critical in keeping practitioners motivated and involved. Connecting to both sides of the organization helped us anticipate the best way to maneuver the work forward, taking into account issues of implementation, union constraints, policy barriers, and a host of workforce issues.

The leaders, with data in hand, worked to build a coalition within each respective institution. The framing of the work was incredibly important to rally support. For SFUSD, it was important to emphasize that examining college readiness was not in addition to our work, but was the core work identified in the strategic plan with a slightly different lens. For CCSF, it was critical to emphasize that the college needed to revisit policies and procedures to examine how they were affecting students of color. In both cases, it was clear that the initiative did not mean we needed to change our missions, but rather emphasized the need to shift the way we thought about our existing work. We increased buy-in by using the data not just as a bunch of numbers but as a way to paint a real and emotional picture about the kids we all served. Sharing students' stories, such as Ruby's, made our case stronger.

Once we developed our message it was time to present the data to as many constituents as possible, a process we called our "road show." Because CCSF has over 100,000 students and thousands of employees, the road show was presented more than forty times at various college committees, departments' shared board meetings, and councils, with some presentations made to the same group more than once, to ensure that the entire college had an understanding of the data and the urgency of necessary change. This road show was important, because CCSF's culture embeds decisions within a shared governance system that would have been impossible to move without this process. SFUSD presented at many different forums that included the superintendent's cabinet, school site principals and assistant principals, central office department leads, lead teachers, and counselors. Presentations were tailored to each audience and created space for reaction and information gathering, but creating a sense of urgency was imperative so that leaders were willing to act now and work toward a solution. The district also met individually with key stakeholders to solicit feedback, which helped create a collaborative solution that made everyone feel they were a part of the decision-making process. Having built support among leaders was critical at this stage, so that presentations to top leadership were not just a cause for alarm but came from a unified staff that had taken the time to develop potential solutions for these concerns.

CONCLUSION

The transition from high school to college occurs between distinctly different institutions, and strong partnerships between these organizations can help students better navigate this challenging time in their lives. This has been the case in San Francisco, where we formed a partnership among the community college, public high school district, and Mayor's Office to tackle these transitional issues. However, partnerships need to go beyond getting leaders into a room. We need to move away from working in isolation, as large bureaucratic institutions often do, toward a more unified approach. Every high school should have a college access strategy, but this strategy will likely only be successful if the colleges meet them halfway. We found the following strategies vital to our progress:

- Partnerships among youth-serving organizations should be attuned to the specific realities in each local community.
- Each institution should assign a practitioner to lead and champion the work at their respective institution.
- Cross-agency partnerships must think carefully about what needs to be accomplished and how it needs to be communicated. We felt that even the small decisions—such as including the names of the

institutional leaders from the two districts and the Mayor's Office on every important e-mail or document that went out—sent an important message that the goals of the initiative were citywide, further emphasizing that these are "our kids."

- Partnerships need to be strategic, intentional, and grounded in data-driven decisions.
- Data should be transparent and presented to all participants in the initiative.
- Recruiting an outside institution to conduct the analysis can help to maintain neutrality and minimize bias.
- Researchers need to proceed at a pace that complements the partners' ongoing responsibilities, and must work hard to explain findings in a clear and concise manner so that the partners understand what can and cannot be interpreted from the data.
- Analyses should be complemented with input from practitioners and those individuals—in our case, students—whom you are intending to help, in order to create a realistic strategic plan.
- It is important to take the necessary time to bring all participants along; the iterative nature of seeing data multiple times can help practitioners understand the results and come up with practical solutions.

We also feel deeply indebted to the Gates Foundation, whose funding in a time of few resources provided the space for these cross-agency conversations and supported the all-important data analysis. In this era of budget cuts, many educational leaders and staff have an overwhelming workload, and questions of "but who will pay for this" and "will we need to pay someone overtime to do this" were immediate inquiries. Outside funding helped alleviate concerns among staff that this initiative was just one more task on their never-ending list of things to do. Having private dollars to finance the initiative also allowed us the flexibility to use the money in creative ways that bypassed strict state regulations on how to expend funds. For example, changes in the law on affirmative action prevent institutions of higher education from serving students based on race, but the private funding allowed us to focus on the ethnic groups that the data revealed to be the students being disproportionately affected by policy barriers. Once it was revealed that funding would not be a problem, we were able to move forward in addressing head-on the issues we cared about.

Although the BtS partnership has shown significant progress toward addressing the access and completion gap, we are well aware that the work has just begun. To that end, our sustainability plan has been incorporated throughout the process, and the third year of this initiative will focus on implementation and institutionalization. We recognized from the beginning that this initiative is really "the work" of our separate institutions, and that this way of working together should become our new norm. We have expressed to site-level staff that this collaboration will become a part of their regular job moving forward, and we have shifted priorities on individual job descriptions to ensure that the work continues to be performed. We are also working on a data-sharing agreement between CCSF and SFUSD that will ensure that we can continue to use linked data to make decisions that benefit our students. Of course, the only pieces of work that will remain from these first years of working together will be the policy and practice changes that the data show have demonstrated an effect on students' lives.

Instead of pointing fingers at each other, we relied on data-driven decisions, and you cannot point fingers at data. This, coupled with powerful student stories such as Ruby's, can create the sense of urgency necessary to change the trajectory of her life—and others like her—toward one that would allow her to participate in the educated citizenry as she deserves.

WHAT RUBY'S STORY COULD HAVE BEEN

The three authors developed this chapter by meeting at various San Francisco cafés, using this time to outline our thoughts and write as a team. While working on the finishing touches, we had a final meeting at a café, when a CCSF student asked to share our table. We had just written about the topic of heavily impacted courses, and we asked her whether she had ever had problems accessing her classes at CCSF. She indicated that she had no problem getting all the courses she needed, but she was not sure that her experience was typical for other students as she was only in her first year at CCSF. Guessing the answer, we asked her where she was the year before, to which she replied, "I just graduated from SFUSD and got an early registration date." Her story adds to our evidence bank that policy changes, such as the early enrollment program, can dramatically impact students' lives by shortening the amount of time it will take to graduate from college and earn a living wage. This example would likely have not had the swift impact or results without a solid, data-driven, cross-institutional partnership. Hearing the direct result of our work in action made a perfect bookend to this chapter.

6

THE REDWOOD CITY
SCHOOL DISTRICT AND
JOHN W. GARDNER CENTER
PARTNERSHIP

Using Integrated Longitudinal Data

Amy Gerstein and Jan Christensen

THE REDWOOD CITY SCHOOL DISTRICT AND JOHN W. GARDNER CENTER

The John W. Gardner Center's (JGC) relationship with the Redwood City School District (RCSD) represents its longest-standing and most developed partnership. Both partners—from leadership through staff members—have worked hard to make this relationship effective and productive. This chapter explores the evolution of this university-district partnership around the Youth Data Archive (YDA), and the lessons we have learned from using data together.

Redwood City is a medium-sized city in the San Francisco Bay Area, adjacent to Silicon Valley, with a population of around 80,000. The local elementary school district, with sixteen schools, serves approximately 9,200 students in grades K–8. The majority of youth attending RCSD schools identify as Latino, approximately half are English language learners, and about two-thirds are on the Free and Reduced Price Lunch program. Many residents are undocumented.

A central element in the JGC's relationship with the district is Redwood City 2020 (RWC 2020), a local collaborative made up of city and county agencies, nonprofits, business leaders, and others with a common goal of supporting the community's youth and families.[1] In 2012, members included the city manager of Redwood City, the executive director of San Mateo County Human Services, the chief medical officer of Kaiser Permanente Hospital in Redwood City, the superintendents of Redwood City School District and Sequoia Union High School District, and the executive director of the Sequoia Healthcare District, among others. Working with representatives of both government and other organizations (primarily nonprofits), RWC 2020 was pivotal in fostering the partnership between the JGC and the RCSD.

In 2005, the Redwood City School District took a leap of faith in joining the YDA initiative as the first data-contributing partner. As members of the first such partnership, both the Gardner Center and the district had to learn how to build and demonstrate trust, though early efforts at using the YDA to conduct research within RCSD proved challenging.

When Superintendent Jan Christensen arrived in the district in 2006, she learned that a preexisting data use agreement between RCSD and the JGC authorized the district to share its student data so that research could be undertaken with various district programs. Although JGC staff worked to clarify the terms—for example, RCSD, like other YDA partners, retains ownership of the data and must agree to all studies and publishing—this arrangement felt unusual to the new superintendent, especially as the school board had not formally approved the agreement. Accordingly, one of the first things Superintendent Christensen did was to send the agreement to the district's counsel to ensure its legality. Upon the expiration of the initial agreement, the RCSD school board approved a new data use agreement.

One Step Back, Two Steps Forward

The first YDA analysis proved problematic for the district. During the 2006–07 school year, the JGC conducted a study examining the English language development of students participating in an afterschool program at the local Boys and Girls Club. Several concerns about the YDA surfaced as a result of the study. It appeared to the district's English language development director and several other district administrators that the study directly correlated attendance at the Boys and Girls Club with increasing students' language acquisition. The primary concern with this inference was that other variables, such as the instruction the students were receiving at school, obstacles (such as cost) to attending the afterschool program, and the district's specific interventions targeted for English language learners were not examined in the YDA analysis. District officials were worried that conclusions reached in that initial study were flawed, and that subsequent articles written by the JGC might well misrepresent the work of the district. Compounding these concerns, there was also a fear that the district could "push back" only so far, because the JGC's then executive director, Craig Baker, also served as a district trustee. Although this issue proved to be more of an apprehension about Baker's potential influence than a reality, as a new superintendent, Christensen was concerned with staff perceptions.

Despite the YDA's rocky start in Redwood City, conversations between the district and the JGC ultimately led to many more constructive discussions about the partnership, which in turn bolstered the relationship with greater trust and allowed subsequent studies to proceed successfully. As the relationship weathered this initial storm, it shifted from one of vague distrust to one of strong mutual trust, and the two entities have since worked collaboratively as partners in youth development. In addition to experience, history also played a role in successfully navigating these initial bumps in the road. Prior to the YDA, the JGC had supported well-regarded work in the district involving youth leadership (Youth Engaged in Leadership and Learning) and the development of a community school model. The JGC's record of positive, strong relationships with the district and RWC 2020 undoubtedly made these conversations, and the patience required to sustain them, possible.

In 2009, JGC's incoming executive director, Amy Gerstein, prioritized relationship development with Redwood City partners. After listening to the district's previous challenges with the YDA and examples of how other prior studies had not always worked, a hope emerged that with attention and positive regard on the part of both partners, trust could further develop. Ultimately, investing the time to develop this relationship paid dividends. In the ensuing years, each of the joint analyses has served to deepen the understanding of key conditions necessary for the work to move forward, as well as factors that can impede success. An essential takeaway from the course of the YDA's history with RCSD is that a productive relationship between community and university partners such as that represented by the YDA does not just happen. Required elements are time, attention, and intentionality, plus, as this case suggests, a positive history that can moderate the fears and distrust peculiar to data.

Growing Together: Listening for Inquiry Opportunities, Identifying Research Questions

Both Gardner Center and the Redwood City School District learned important lessons from that first analysis. On the JGC side, we learned how important it was to ensure that partners were invested in and poised to respond to the findings from an analysis from the start. For RCSD, it was important to see that lines of communication could be open and that their concerns would be heard and responded to by YDA researchers. The growing confidence in the Gardner Center's role as a neutral third party resulted in an increased willingness to examine issues within the district for which a research approach might provide information and possible solutions. A partner-driven research approach requires that researchers listen critically to partners' concerns; understanding the issues with which partners struggle provides clues to ways that data might illuminate areas for inquiry. Moving forward from the afterschool participation analysis and leveraging the heightened level of mutual trust, YDA researchers worked with the district and other community partners to identify additional areas of inquiry that might prove helpful.

Shared areas of concern soon emerged. Specifically, the district, the San Mateo County Health System, and other partners expressed an interest in understanding youth health outcomes in the context of their academic achievement. The YDA team engaged in a longitudinal analysis of students' educational outcomes and their physical fitness as measured by the California physical fitness test taken in fifth, seventh, and ninth grades. This analysis combined data from both RCSD and the Sequoia Union High School District, which enrolls the largest number of RCSD graduates (see chapter 3 for a full description of this study). This YDA analysis represented the first time elementary and high school district data had been linked to look longitudinally at students' pathways.

SEEKING ACTIONABLE KNOWLEDGE, BUILDING CAPACITY: THE COMMUNITY SCHOOLS INITIATIVE

With the Gardner Center's support, RCSD pioneered the community school model in northern California, and district staff were eager for evidence about how it was working and might be improved. Redwood City's six community schools bring together many partners to offer a range of supports and opportunities to children, youth, families, and communities. After three years of working with an outside evaluation firm, the district turned to the JGC to study its community schools. District educators were unhappy with the evaluator's results because the generally laudatory evaluation reports neither matched their experience nor informed their practice. Specifically, the district sought to understand which particular programs and practices in community schools most benefited student learning outcomes and supported families. To that end, YDA researchers used the archive to identify patterns associated with community schools and to provide the district with actionable research.

YDA staff analyzed administrative data from schools and the multiple programs and services in which students and their parents participated. Researchers then provided the district with written reports and briefs regarding the community schools each year. Using linked data from the YDA, researchers documented how participation in community school programming related to various educational outcomes—from attendance, to discipline, to achievement, to English language development. Given the longitudinal nature of these analyses, a complex picture of effects emerged.[2]

The community schools project not only resulted in findings that could shape decisions and policy at school and district levels, it also provided an opportunity for capacity building within the district. YDA staff and district leadership led joint discussions with the practitioners at each site; an explicit and shared goal of this process was to build the capacity of key players in the district to understand and utilize data. YDA staff met with principals, community school coordinators, and teachers at individual school sites explaining data findings, answering questions, and discussing implications of the research. These "data talks" assisted school staff in implementing effective teaching practices—particularly those that demonstrated increased student achievement. And as a result of these sessions, Redwood City teachers and administrators as well as community stakeholders developed increased sophistication in posing nuanced questions related to their work. Rather than asking whether an initiative is resulting in positive outcomes, they are now asking, "In what ways is this family engagement program working and why does it appear to have effects when combined with extended learning? How can we use these findings to improve our work?"

In the course of the community schools study, YDA staff also worked closely with the district to improve its data collection strategies so that it would have the pertinent data to answer important questions about community schools practice. For example, early in the process of working with the community schools, YDA researchers helped providers to develop common metrics of participation. Previously, some programs collected daily attendance and others only kept a list of participants. This uneven data gathering inhibited the collective capacity to answer questions about the effects of frequency of participation on student outcomes. Over time, community providers agreed to adopt and use a common data system for collecting more detailed participation data. With better participation data, the district learned about patterns of access to services. Through analysis of who accessed which kinds of services and who did not access any services, the district learned a great deal about outreach and targeting that prompted district leaders to develop strategies for outreach to subgroups that never accessed services. District-level data broadened leaders' perspective by displaying patterns and trends beyond individual schools. Looking holistically at the district enabled its leadership to develop systemic strategies focusing on cross-site work.

The YDA community schools study also engaged new actors in the work and deepened community partnerships. The research clearly showed the value of support services for students' academic outcomes and families' participation. As a result, the district's leadership adopted an informal philosophy that all its sixteen schools should function as community schools. The district's director of community-school partnerships now works with all principals to offer students and families support services. One way in which this has occurred is through leveraging the district's partnership with Redwood City's Parks and Recreation Department to offer programs and services in a coordinated fashion at the school sites. The improvements in data collection, capacity building, and research findings provided by the YDA have helped RCSD to advance its community school strategy and to deepen its local partnerships to better serve its students.

USING YDA RESEARCH TO SUPPORT ACTION

The Youth Data Archive has supported policy change in RCSD, leveraged new partnerships, and contributed to the district's capacity to collect and use data. Critical to these results was the partners' buy-in to and ownership of the research questions. For instance, even though California's budget crisis constrained response to the YDA's analysis of the relationship between physical fitness and academics, district commitment to acting on the findings as a strategy to enhance students' school outcomes led to an array of productive responses. More than three years after the analysis on fitness and achievement concluded, RCSD continues to incorporate the findings into policies and practices. At a policy level, school board member Shelly Masur advocated the inclusion of physical fitness strategies to increase student achievement in the district's formal, mandated comprehensive Local Educational Agency (LEA) plan submitted to the state in 2011. This past spring, the superintendent disseminated articles to site principals that highlighted the value of having students exercise immediately prior to taking achievement tests.

Moreover, the district recently sought to leverage its partnership with the local Sequoia Healthcare District, an RWC 2020 member, to further capitalize on the link between physical fitness and achievement. For two years the Sequoia Healthcare District funded several area school districts as part of its Healthy Schools Initiative. This included funding several nurses for RCSD, a counselor, and a wellness coordinator. The Sequoia Healthcare District also allocated funds to another organization, the nonprofit Serve the Peninsula, to provide several district elementary schools with direct physical education instruction. In 2012, the Sequoia Healthcare District expanded its collaboration with the school district and Serve the Peninsula by funding additional physical education and part-time athletic coaches for RCSD elementary schools in addition to funding its Healthy Schools Initiative.

The YDA's chronic absenteeism study commissioned by Redwood City 2020 partners provides another example of how stakeholders' shared questions can prompt action (see chapter 4 for a study description). The topic of truancy and chronic absenteeism and their effects on student performance was generated by the RWC 2020's cabinet out of concerns about truancy and its possible relationship to a variety of issues with which partners were grappling. For example, both districts were especially interested to learn about the scope of the problem and which students were chronically truant. The County Health System, the local hospital, and the Sequoia Healthcare District wanted to know about the relationship between absenteeism and health indicators. The correlation between absenteeism and public assistance was of particular interest to the Human Services Agency. Together the collaborative partners looked to the YDA to study the issue and to help identify areas that the community might address in concert. The YDA staff helped clarify the questions for the partners to ensure that the research would be both actionable and focused on the problems about which the partners were most concerned.

Despite high rates of average daily attendance (ADA) in both districts, the findings uncovered important areas for support and intervention. Even though the study has not yet been formally presented to the RCSD school board, the district has already taken action. The RCSD superintendent was concerned over preliminary results that pointed to the high rates of early chronic absenteeism in kindergarten. Given the evidence that this pattern might become a prognostic indicator of chronic absenteeism at other grade levels and have a clear and negative effect on student achievement, she directed principals to focus on kindergartners who are frequently absent. Due to the diminishing capacity of the Redwood City school-site office staff, principally due to budget cuts, the absenteeism letters were not always sent out in a timely manner. But the district has now contracted with an outside vendor to monitor student absences and issue correspondence to parents whose students are frequently absent, and it has budgeted for an attendance coordinator in the 2012–13 school year.

This research will also leverage new conversations among community agencies. For example, the next steps for this effort involve bringing together the various health-care providers to discuss the findings. These providers may inadvertently contribute to absenteeism by repeatedly excusing youth with chronic illnesses without understanding the broader picture of attendance problems. The outreach effort to these health-care providers is to be facilitated by the membership of the RWC 2020 cabinet, which includes Kaiser Permanente Hospital and the Sequoia Healthcare District. Additionally, the local juvenile justice system will be engaged in conversation about the findings, which also identified systemic issues related to student truancy and disconnects between the juvenile justice and school systems. Finally, RWC 2020 will convene a multi-agency group and a cross-role team from within the district to learn more about the study and to develop interventions to address the issue. Responses to this study by community partners highlight the influence a research effort can have when it responds to questions deemed urgent by users.

CHALLENGES TO COMMUNITY-UNIVERSITY PARTNERSHIP

Benefits of the partnership between RCSD and JGC's Youth Data Archive have been many and have resulted in a wealth of learning, policy change, and improvement in practice. Both community and university partners have grown and explored new ways of working across traditional boundaries and roles. This collaborative work has also revealed challenges endemic to a community-university partnership based in research. They range in kind from personal to political to cultural to technical.

Managing Different Priorities

The YDA team is clear that the primary purpose of their work with RCSD is to improve and support the district and its schools. However, priorities for both partners also may differ. For example, university-based researchers value publications in academic journals and presentations to scholarly conferences, goals which require research that meets academic standards of rigor. Community stakeholders may be impatient with analyses that seem too theoretical or that make methodological demands such as a sufficient sample size. YDA researchers juggle multiple priorities in managing the academy, adhering to the partnership agreements, and grappling with the demands of research and the standards of intellectual freedom.

The JCG has responded to this ongoing challenge in several ways. YDA researchers produce community-oriented products from the analyses first, so that partners can see, approve, and use the findings before any more academic publications or presentations are developed. The community-oriented products are based on the same high standards of research as those produced for an academic audience, but they may not respond as well to the broader literature because they focus specifically on the issues and concerns of the community. Where appropriate, other products that are oriented more to the academy are developed later with more in-depth or sophisticated analyses and techniques. However, it is often the case that in order to accurately report on issues identified by partners, YDA researchers, while always using sophisticated analysis techniques, do make efforts to present the information to community partners in simpler ways that resonate with the questions those partners asked.

Managing Differential Pace of Work

A shared commitment to producing actionable knowledge undergirds the YDA partnership with the district, but the pace of action is not always shared or aligned. Schools and districts manage thousands of children each day. Myriad moving parts need attention ranging from human to facility to political and technical problems to solve. At any given moment an urgent need might trump all planning and commandeer the focus of the school or district leadership. Decisions in districts need to be made quickly and are often unanticipated.

University researchers strive to understand their partners' culture and context but live in a different world. Once the relatively long process of defining a research question is completed, and data are gathered, the subsequent analysis can take months. Understanding the relevant and actionable story in the findings takes time. Communicating with schools and the district takes time. The amount of time involved in this research process can seem luxurious and painstaking at times to some partners in the field. YDA researchers, on the other hand, sometimes feel rushed and pressured to conduct high-quality work within tight time constraints, else the research will be too late to be useful. Managing this differential pace poses a challenge inherent to this research partnership.

The community schools research illustrates this tension. When district leaders were in a planning and decision-making mode relative to community schools resource allocation, they needed data quickly in order to understand if there were measurable student effects that could justify funding the community school coordinator positions. The administration needed evidence. Budgets needed approval. Yet linking data from multiple sources and analyzing those data took time. The sophisticated statistical models the YDA researchers used to study the issues required sufficient time to understand the results.

The differential pace of the work is sometimes further affected by the technical difficulties of data transfer. The amalgamation process of garnering, cleaning, and matching data across institutions is time-consuming and demands careful attention. In the course of the chronic absenteeism study the YDA team experienced some pressure to hurry. The complexity of the research model demanded sufficient time, but the interagency team from RWC 2020 was eager to learn about findings and to build an action plan. The JGC's executive director served as the intermediary to understand the nature of everyone's concerns and the YDA team provided interim findings as a strategy to manage these expectations for quick results. However, as is often the case with research efforts, the picture changed as the final analysis developed, and this created some confusion among some of the partners. Despite strong relationships, frustration can result from the disparate pace of work among community and university partners and from the potential lack of understanding about the pressures involved in one another's work. Frequent communication between the researchers and the RWC 2020 cabinet leadership helped to mitigate these obstacles.

Managing Differences in Language

When YDA staff reported interim findings of the chronic absenteeism study to the RWC 2020 cabinet, it became apparent that some community partners did not understand some of the research vocabulary. YDA staff had used terms such as "regression analysis" or "statistically significant" for years and assumed there was shared understanding. Yet the chronic absenteeism presentation demonstrated that many colleagues appeared confused as YDA staff explained preliminary findings to partners from multiple agencies. YDA researchers needed to stop and think about vocabulary anew and take into consideration that not all the members of RWC 2020 have had the same number of years on the cabinet, or the same exposure to research.

Realizing that partners may not understand a fundamental research technique or terminology that the YDA utilized in previous presentations prompted staff to reflect on possible communication gaps. The community partners in turn questioned the presentation and its meaning where things were unclear. This back-and-forth exemplified the confident relationship existing between the partners and YDA researchers. All parties felt comfortable enough to ask one another clarifying questions. The lead researcher on that analysis provided many stopping points at each briefing, checking for understanding and to invite comments and questions.

Limitations of Administrative Data

Each YDA analysis generates at least as many questions as it answers. Sometimes these questions are unanswerable using the data that the district or other partners provided. Despite the many benefits of longitudinal, integrated data, these data also have limitations, as chapter 7 elaborates. For instance, the administrative data that informed the community schools analyses could not address questions about program quality. Nor could they answer questions regarding why families were participating or not in community school activities. Complementing these studies with qualitative research will provide a more complete picture and may lead to greater opportunities for improvement. But answering these questions with "more research is needed" is only part of the solution. Understanding the limits prior to engaging in the analysis would help the partners up front. Setting expectations in advance might well support better inquiry.

Garnering Sufficient Resources to Support the Work

Supporting the university-community partnership work with adequate resources has been a struggle for RCSD and JGC since the beginning. The JGC decided early in its work with RCSD to invest resources—time, money, and human capital—into the partnership for the long term. For JGC, investing core operational resources was vital both in showing its commitment and in demonstrating that analyses based on integrated, longitudinal data could lead to better policies for a community's young people. Key JGC leadership committed time to working in the community to build relationships and capacity; the JGC invested significant dollars and staff to make this work.

After seven years of partnership, Redwood City partners, including the school district, began to assist in paying for some of the research. In addition to this monetary contribution, partners continued to dedicate significant resources in terms of staff time to participate in the work. Finding grant makers who understand the nature of this unusual work presents significant challenges, however. The fiscal climate in California further decreased the few extant public dollars available for supporting the

YDA. Using research from this partnership has helped RCSD to allocate resources more effectively, thus justifying its commitment to the YDA. This pay-for-service model is the way the YDA is moving forward in other communities, relying on grants received by community partners or collaboratives that include a research component. Monetary commitment to support the research is important for both the sustainability of the YDA and for the investment of community partners. Partners will only pay for research that they are committed to using, and these payments make them accountable to the research process and invested in its outcomes.

LESSONS LEARNED

As RCSD's relationship with the JGC through the Youth Data Archive initiative grows, we have reflected on earlier experiences—both positive and challenging—to improve our processes of communication, capacity building, reporting, and actionability. This concluding section offers lessons learned from our partnership and the first test site for the YDA.

Relationship Building and Trust

The partnership with JGC required more of the district superintendent than an understanding of research. It required establishing a trusting relationship across the whole district and with the JGC. Likewise, JGC and YDA staff had to work in a manner that did not create distrust of the research or the researchers. Some districts and their superintendents and school boards are reluctant to participate in any type of "outside" research because researchers have used research results to provide harsh critiques of districts and their practices. The relationship established and maintained between the JGC and RCSD over the past seven years has shown that the YDA can be trusted to keep data safe and confidential and to share findings only when all parties agree they are ready to do so.

Superintendents desiring to engage in research partnerships such as the YDA need to spend sufficient time in building strong, open relationships with the researchers before these partnerships can be successful. As the RCSD superintendent and the JGC executive director, we have committed personal time beyond our workdays to meet and discuss issues. We have bimonthly dinner meetings to discuss myriad issues revolving around the work of both entities. Putting in the time to get to know one another and establishing these common goals, commitments, values, and aspirations goes a long way toward coping with the inevitable frustrations of partnership and collaboration. Without such a commitment, both of us doubt this type of partnership could continue to sustain itself in the long term.

Expectations and Embedded Agreements

Superintendents typically leave the position after three years. School board trustees' tenures are also dynamic. New superintendents or trustees may feel differently or know nothing about the district's partnerships with researchers. A change in leadership at the superintendent level should not mean that the commitment of the policy makers to a YDA partnership has shifted. Formal data use agreements provide stability, as does establishing partnership expectations at the time a new leader is hired. Also critical to the smooth operation of a YDA is leadership's authoritative communication to middle management responsible for data transfer that working with the YDA partners and responding to their data requests is an important part of their job, not an add-on.

Responsible Partnership Policies

The YDA's individually linked, cross-agency, longitudinal data represent an unusual resource for districts. YDA analyses allow districts to look across institutional boundaries and consider the broader youth context, to identify relationships and opportunities otherwise not evident. But data such as those contained in the YDA as part of a university partnership also represent a potential threat. The YDA's policy that all data contributors have "review and approve" authority before research is published allows RCSD's open-handed participation, thus enabling the generation of new knowledge both for the district and for the youth-serving field more generally.

Promises of Engaging in Actionable Research

Much of what binds the district and the JGC together are their shared commitments and goals with regard to youth development. A common interest in improved outcomes for youth and families drives the ongoing work, while the mutual respect for one another's expertise enables success. One of the many shared interests has been the promise of engaging in actionable research—the belief that the research will result in something tangibly better for kids. The accountability era of the last fifteen years has yielded data and analyses that have produced punitive results rather than positive action. For Redwood City, the promise of participating in research that would provide answers to their own questions and move their local agenda forward propelled their engagement.

Importance of Collaboratives

At the center of the Redwood City YDA work is an intermediary organization, Redwood City 2020. Formed in 1995, RWC 2020 has responded to the diminishing resources available to the community's young people by convening a cross-agency collaborative of executive leaders to identify ways to focus on youth development issues.[3] RWC 2020 has been an essential resource in convening local youth-serving agencies and organizations, brokering knowledge among them, providing a context for identifying shared research questions, and supporting the YDA's involvement in the community and data needs.

7

BEYOND ADMINISTRATIVE DATA

Using Multiple Methods to Study
Youth Outcomes

Karen Strobel, Sebastian Castrechini, and Lisa Westrich

INTRODUCTION

The preceding chapters of this book focus on Youth Data Archive (YDA) research that links administrative data collected by partner agencies. However, our partners often ask questions that are difficult, or impossible, to answer with administrative data alone. This chapter focuses on two studies that utilized YDA data in combination with additional data sources. One project linked YDA data to supplement data from a survey of middle school students. The survey asks students about their motivational beliefs and their experiences in their middle school classrooms. John W. Gardner Center (JGC) researchers have administered this survey in classrooms throughout the Redwood City School District each spring since 2009. A separate project supplemented YDA analyses on the benefits of attending community schools in the district (see chapter 6) with qualitative data collection. Our research team interviewed school-based staff, parents, and students about their perceptions of family engagement at their schools.

There are three types of data sources that are typically used in our data analyses: administrative, survey, and qualitative. Administrative data consist of information collected *about* youth; this is the type of data that are stored in agency databases and that the YDA links across agencies. For instance, school administrative data include information such as student demographics, attendance, and test scores. Survey data are collected directly *from* youth. They tend to capture less observable characteristics, such as students' attitudes about school or behaviors outside the classroom, but they typically do so with closed-ended statements for participants to respond to with predetermined response options. Like administrative data, survey data are tabulated and analyzed using quantitative methods. Qualitative data generally consist of longer narratives captured in the voice of participants, usually from individual interviews or focus groups. Because collecting these data is more time-intensive, they are usually collected from a sample, or subset, of the population that researchers want to study.

Administrative data are not always sufficient to answer the questions partners have about the youth they serve. For example, administrative data are good at quantifying inputs (such as attendance and program participation) and their relationship to outputs (such as test scores, grades, or graduation), but they generally do not offer much insight into the processes or reasons behind observed links. Reporting or accountability requirements often dictate decisions about which data are collected and so limit data options. As a result, data collected for these purposes may not be sufficient to fully answer the research questions that partners would like to have answered. Additionally, administrative data may not speak directly to practitioners' experiences and thus may feel unusable to them. For example, although test scores are often reported in media and research reports, they may not align with the pedagogical or curriculum questions that teachers have about their own practice. Administrative data may dictate action at the policy level, but they are not inherently actionable at the practice level.

This chapter explores two projects that have supplemented YDA research with survey and qualitative data. Through these case studies we provide examples of the complementary relationship between YDA administrative data and supplemental data. We conclude with some lessons and considerations in conducting supplemental data collection.

CASE STUDIES

In this section we describe how the two cases emerged and discuss key findings and action steps. These details provide important background to better understand both the benefits and challenges of supplementing the YDA with additional data collection.

Youth Development Survey

Background   In 2000 the Gardner Center created the Youth Engaged in Leadership and Learning (YELL) program in response to requests from the Redwood City 2020 collaborative to capture students' perspectives on ways schools and community programs could better meet the needs of youth.[1] What started off as a short-term community mapping project transformed into an afterschool program providing leadership development training for sixth-, seventh-, and eighth-grade students at one middle school. As the program unfolded, JGC researchers documented both program and student development over time. The research did not serve as a program evaluation; rather, it allowed for an exploration of what youth leadership can look like and the range of program practices that promote youth leadership.

As researchers captured participants' leadership development and motivation to engage in change processes at school and in the community, community partners became interested in ways to connect and align afterschool experiences with school-day experiences. Working together with district personnel, JGC staff developed the Youth in the Middle (YiM) project to engage teachers, administrators, and afterschool staff at two RCSD schools in a process of envisioning and implementing a whole-school youth development approach. A youth development approach recognizes the importance of emotional, social, and physical growth in addition to intellectual development. Moreover, a youth development approach focuses on students' strengths rather than only addressing risks or problems, seeking to create the conditions and promote practices that support developmental processes.

A full year was devoted to brainstorming, articulating issues, and learning together through workshops. At the end of that first year, the visioning team of administrators, teachers, and afterschool staff articulated the following schoolwide goals:

- Creating a supportive and caring community
- Supporting youth voice, input, and autonomy
- Motivating students to engage in their learning

At the request of the YiM team, JGC researchers began to develop a student survey that mapped onto the schools' goals for creating a caring and motivating school that supported youth voice. The YiM team hoped to use the survey to capture students' perspectives and inform their efforts. Initially, JGC researchers planned to administer a schoolwide survey at one middle school that had been involved in both YELL and YiM. Over the course of the 2008–09 academic year, the JGC executive director spoke with principals from other RCSD schools who also expressed interest in administering a survey that would capture students' beliefs about learning as well as their perceptions of classroom practices. With multiple schools expressing interest, the JGC executive director and the superintendent discussed the benefit of a districtwide youth development survey. In the end, RCSD invited the JGC to administer a survey to all sixth-through eighth-grade students across nine schools in the district.

Approval process   Before a districtwide survey could be approved, administrators and the teachers union needed assurance that the data would be collected, analyzed, and disseminated in ways that would not harm the reputation of individual teachers, schools, or the district as a whole. Other YDA projects include data use agreements in which the JGC and partnering agencies sign a legally binding document outlining how the data can and cannot be used. Because we planned to collect new data for this project, our team needed to make it clear that the district still had authority over how that data would be collected, analyzed, and shared. For example, we agreed that the JGC would develop survey items, but the district would review and approve of all questions included in the final version of the student survey. The JGC agreed to not share raw data with anyone outside of the JGC and to not share individual classroom- or school-level results in any report unless specifically requested by the district. JGC researchers also promised to not identify individual students or teachers in any reports, publications, or presentations. Furthermore, we agreed that the district must review and approve all written materials and presentations. Through these agreements, district administrators recognized that they owned the data even though JGC was responsible for the data collection.

The teachers union, however, was not as comfortable with the proposed data collection.

We needed to assure the union that we would protect the identities of teachers and not use the data to target teachers who were not implementing youth development practices in their classrooms. At the request of the teachers union, we rephrased all survey items to make sure the word "teacher" was not included. Questions about ways teachers show they care about students proved challenging to rephrase. For example, "My math teacher talks with me about things going on in my life," was rephrased as, "In math class I have a chance to talk about how things are going in my life." This revision clearly changed the meaning of the question, but it succeeded in addressing the teachers union's concerns. However, because the wording was changed, responses to these questions were no longer comparable to the original survey questions and generalizable to the research literature stemming from them.

Connecting back to the three goals that the YiM visioning team set, approved survey questions and analyses focused on students' perceptions of care and support at school and in the classroom, the degree to which students feel they have a voice in their classrooms, and the extent to which students feel motivated to engage in their learning. In addition to representing partners' interests, these three areas align with an established motivation theory, known as self-determination theory, which says that youth who satisfy their needs for having a voice and autonomy (self-determination), feeling connected to others (relatedness), and feeling confident in their abilities (competence) are more likely to improve their engagement in school and their achievement as well.[12] We measured feeling connected to others in terms of classroom-wide strategies to create a climate of respect because it was not possible to ask about relationships with teachers without using the word "teacher."

By connecting our local work to the broader field of motivation and youth development, our team provided an important resource to our partners. In addition to providing data about classroom practices and students' beliefs, we were able to provide well-established theoretical frameworks as guides for the questions we included in the survey as well as the research questions we posed in our analyses. A theoretically guided data collection allows teachers and administrators to understand how and why their practices matter for their students. At the same time, a connection to theory can help generate ideas that our partners can apply to their local reality.

Logistics In the spring of 2009 the JGC team administered the first youth development survey to all 2,300 sixth- through eighth-grade students in RCSD. Access to administrative data through the YDA greatly facilitated survey administration. Using archive records, the YDA team generated fictitious identification numbers for each student linked to their district identification number. On the day of survey administration, JGC researchers entered each classroom with a list of students' names and a survey identification number for each student. These identification numbers were a critical component of the survey process because they linked the survey data to the YDA without requiring students to put their name or their real student number on the survey. This strategy was important for making students feel comfortable in knowing that their survey answers were confidential. This system also allowed us to link the survey responses to all of the demographic and academic information that we had in the YDA. The identification number system allowed us to shorten the survey because we did not have to ask students basic demographic questions, such as their grade or gender, as we could obtain this information from the YDA.

Buy-in Findings from the first year of data collection focused on specific practices in the classroom which influenced students' competence beliefs. When we shared analyses with the practitioners, we failed to build a convincing argument for emphasizing students' beliefs as an outcome of interest. Our framework and our presentation to principals focused on the relationship between youth development practices and students' competence beliefs. The principals, in contrast, were focused on achievement outcomes, so our emphasis on competence beliefs seemed tangential and irrelevant to them. Moreover, the school-specific summaries of certain practices did not match practitioners' experiences in those schools. In one school in which students' performed poorly on standardized achievement tests in math and English, survey responses portrayed the school as highly caring. In our model, caring practices were associated with positive competence beliefs, which were precursors to achievement. However, this finding did not make sense to our partners and did not match with perceptions of this school and evidence of students' academic struggles.

The framework for our findings appeared to our partners to have been imposed on them. At one meeting when the research team was sharing findings from the student survey, observers documented phrases such as "this is an imposition, these are outsiders, constructs [are] irrelevant in this budget crisis, data do not match what [we] know to be the truth." The main line of their narrative was "since you can't trust the data, there's not much you can do." Our analyses seemed particularly irrelevant during a time of significant pressure to improve scores on standardized tests. Moreover, the principals with whom we shared findings had not been part of the original "visioning team" that articulated goals for creating caring communities, motivating students, and supporting youth voice.

As the spring of 2010 approached, the district was not ready to commit to another round of data collection. As one district administrator said, "If I don't know what to do with this data, then [I am] not sure why [I] want more." Our research team needed to revisit the original goals of the survey and the questions the district hoped we would address. With the help of a new executive director at the JGC, the research team worked with the superintendent to better match the analysis with questions that were meaningful for the schools. Leveraging the YDA data providing academic histories for each student, we focused on indicators from the survey data that predicted achievement. Our new analytic framework focused on how promoting students' competence, beliefs, and goals for learning and improvement had the potential to improve students' scores on standardized achievement tests (see figure 7.1).

With renewed interest from the district, we administered a revised youth development survey in the spring of 2010. The survey revisions responded to feedback from students, teachers, and principals about the length of the survey and particularly confusing questions. For example, the original survey included questions about how students regulated their emotions when they were in school. They were asked to rate how much they agreed with statements such as "You can learn to control your emotions" and "When I'm faced with a stressful situation, I make myself think about it in a way that helps me stay calm." Students felt that these questions were too personal. In addition, questions that included negative statements, such as "In math class nothing less than my full effort is accepted" and "When I want to feel less negative emotion, I change what I'm thinking about," proved challenging for students to answer using the scaled responses ranging from "not true of me" to "very true of me." In response to concerns about length of the survey and difficult questions, we cut more than half of the survey questions to allow us to minimize the loss of instructional time and also minimize confusion or frustration among the students.

In addition to revising the content of the survey, our team also worked closely with principals and school staff to revise the process of administering the survey. Each school took ownership of the data collection process,

Figure 7.1 Pathway to achievement

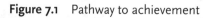

determining the schedule that worked best and taking responsibility for communicating the plan to their teachers. For example, a few schools decided that the best plan was to survey all students during first period. This required up to ten JGC researchers to administer surveys in all middle school classrooms simultaneously. Other schools preferred that we survey students during physical education or language arts classes throughout the course of the school day.

Key findings　After several years of survey data collection, analyses focused on competence beliefs as predictors of achievement and identified classroom practices that cultivated those beliefs. We found that students from all demographic backgrounds who felt competent and believed they could master their schoolwork were more likely to score higher on standardized achievement tests. Also, classroom practices that encouraged effort and understanding and created a caring learning environment were linked to increased student motivation to learn and, ultimately, to higher achievement. Moreover, we found that students' motivational beliefs were malleable and responsive to changes in classroom practices from one year to the next.

Multiple years of survey data allowed us to take into account students' motivational histories as well as their academic histories to help isolate the role that specific practices played in promoting motivation and achievement. The YDA enabled a much more accurate picture of each student as well as what their classrooms and schools are like. When combined with survey responses, these details from administrative data resulted in a much more complex and perhaps complete analysis of students' experiences.

The survey data also has enriched other YDA analyses. In our research on RCSD's community schools (see chapter 6), we used the survey data to understand the links between participation in services at community schools and student achievement. In the early years of the analysis, we began to see relationships between participation in a few program areas at the community schools and academic achievement scores, but we had no way of understanding why. After discussion with our partners, we acknowledged the need to examine shorter-term outcomes, and the director of school-community partners developed a logic model that placed school connectedness as a short-term outcome of community school services connected to the longer-term outcome of improved achievement. Using survey data matched to student administrative data and participation records from the service providers at community schools from the YDA, we found that students with consistent family participation in family engagement opportunities coupled with extended learning showed significant improvement in their reported sense of care at school, and sense of care was a strong predictor of achievement. Also, linking additional survey data from afterschool programs, we found a relationship between students' experiences in afterschool programs and their survey results in school. These findings illuminated two processes through which the community schools affect achievement and helped the community school partners talk about promoting specific practices at the community school programs to foster students' sense of care.

Post-analysis action steps   The survey data has opened the doors for important conversations about schoolwide and classroom-specific practices. The YDA allows us to look at the data at an aggregate level, analyze data districtwide, protect the confidentiality of individual students, teachers, and schools, and, at the same time, provide meaningful and relevant information. Because we are embedded in the community and in the district, our analyses invite the district to recognize that we are reflecting back to them practices that are happening in their school district and highlighting those that seem to be working. For example, our analyses provided evidence of the relationship between caring practices and students' motivation and achievement, and teachers used the data as a catalyst for discussing strategies for identifying and reaching out to the students who have not developed strong ties to their school community.

As we have engaged the schools in discussing the data, teachers and administrators have become increasingly interested in the survey results and have taken ownership of the data. Initial survey findings encouraged our partners to ask more questions of the data and request additional survey items. Our survey initially asked students about practices that create a caring and respectful classroom. In subsequent conversations with teachers, they shared with us debates they had about whether it was more important to care about students emotionally or to show care by supporting students academically. In response to their inquiries, the next year we added items to our survey to explore the multiple ways in which teachers can show students that they care. Moreover, teachers pointed to the importance of including the word "teacher" in the questions to more accurately capture students' perceptions of their interactions with their teachers. The request to include the word "teacher" is noteworthy, given initial requests to take it out of the survey, and is a sign that we had earned their trust over the course of this process. Principals also drafted school-specific questions that we added to their school's surveys; at one school we worked together to compose open-ended questions that students answered with written responses (as opposed to circling a number to indicate agreement with a statement).

Qualitative Study of Family Engagement in Community Schools

Background   The JGC has been engaged in a multiyear partnership with RCSD and Redwood City 2020 to examine community school program participation and student outcomes in five Redwood City schools using the YDA. In RCSD, five schools have been designated as community schools, or schools that partner with service providers to provide a range of extended learning, family engagement, and social support services coordinated through the school. The theory behind community schools is that utilizing partnerships to provide wraparound services for students and families reduces barriers to learning and strengthens connections between students and their families and the school.[2,3] The five RCSD community schools include two K–8 elementary schools, two K–5 schools, and a 6–8 middle school, all serving majority Latino and low-income students and sharing the common strategies of intentional integration of services for students and families through community partnerships.

A main finding over our four years of research is a consistent relationship between family engagement and student achievement. Students whose parents participated in family engagement opportunities consistently across multiple years tended to improve significantly in their achievement scores compared to students with no family engagement participation, particularly in English language development scores for English language learners. These findings raised further questions about practices related to family engagement. When we presented and discussed findings, the director of school-community partnerships and community school coordinators wanted to know more about the relationship between family engagement and achievement. They asked what the family engagement programs, such as parent education classes and school leadership trainings for parents, were doing that might be explaining these achievement gains in order to think about how other program areas can similarly support student achievement. Also, looking at participation numbers and participant characteristics raised questions among the partners. First, the director noted that family engagement at school is broader than counting program attendance, which is how the YDA captures engagement. Community school coordinators also looked at parent participation numbers and sometimes felt that what was captured in the YDA was lower than reality because many of the informal ways that parents engage at school were not included in program participation records. In addition, community school coordinators wanted to understand the factors inhibiting engagement for parents and the practices that programs or schools used to facilitate family engagement.

We realized that we had reached the limit of what YDA data could tell us and that we would need to collect qualitative data in order to answer these questions. With the support of the superintendent and director of school-community partnerships, we sought a grant to conduct a qualitative study of family engagement in the RCSD community schools.

Approving a new data collection strategy   In contrast to the student motivation survey, the family engagement study was directly initiated by RCSD. Our partners in RCSD saw the JGC research team as an important resource for exploring the deeper questions raised by the YDA analyses and better understanding how to improve their family engagement practices. The director was particularly interested in exploring the validity of different family engagement models she had been reading about and in learning how current community school practices were aligned with those frame-works. In response to their request for a supplemental study to the YDA re-search, the team drafted a qualitative study design and worked closely with school staff, including a community school coordinator from each school, to plan data collection efforts. Our team made revisions to the study de-sign and adjusted the data collection plans based on feedback from part-ners. For example, we initially planned to conduct two focus groups with parents at each school in the study. At the suggestion of the coordinators, we interviewed one group of parent leaders who were identified as "en-gaged" by the coordinators and a separate group of parents who were re-cruited from the broad school population. We included in the analyses an additional school site that had recently become a community school, and we also interviewed additional program staff in response to partner input.

Logistics Through this process we learned that even in cases where the district initiates and supports the study, it can be logistically challenging to recruit participants. In each school, the community school coordina-tor served as the key liaison for coordinating participation in interviews and focus groups as well as being participants in the study themselves. Although the study team developed selection criteria for participation in interviews, each school engaged in slightly different processes for recruit-ing teachers, program staff, parents, and students for interviews. In some schools a simple e-mail from a researcher saying that "the principal sug-gested that I contact you" or "the coordinator suggested that I contact you" was sufficient for recruiting staff members. In other schools, the researcher had less direct contact with interview candidates and was forced to rely on the school-based staff to coordinate the logistics. Although it was gener-ous of the school staff to take on the responsibility, in the end it did not al-ways prove to be efficient or reliable. The greatest challenge was recruiting parents who, by definition and design for the study, were not typically en-gaged in the school. Our team offered dinner, child care, and a gift card as incentives for participation. At some schools we had to turn parents away while at other schools we struggled to gather a group of more than three parents. We suspect that in schools where parents had strong relationships with the coordinator and principal, parents were more open and interested in supporting the school through participation. These schools also tended to have organized systems for reaching out to parents and to be supportive of the study.

Buy-in   In addition to the support of district-level staff who requested the qualitative study, buy-in from the community school coordinators was critical. The research team was invited to a coordinator meeting to introduce the study in the early phase of the design process. This strategy gave the research team an opportunity to explain why the study was requested, what the data collection process would look like, and how the findings could make a direct contribution to their work. It also gave the coordinators an opportunity to ask questions, make suggestions, and discuss together how the study was aligned to their current work. Fostering a positive relationship with the coordinators paved the way for being welcomed into the schools and gaining support from principals. Overall, school and program staff were willing participants in the research study and were appreciative of the opportunity to voice their opinions and contribute to the study. Parents who participated in the focus groups also expressed their appreciation for the chance to share their experiences and perspectives.

Key findings   This project is still in progress. However, we anticipate that the qualitative findings will enrich the quantitative YDA analysis by providing insights into the conditions necessary for strong family engagement and the obstacles to engagement as well as strategies to overcome those obstacles. The interview data also offer teachers, principals, and program providers a voice and an opportunity to look beyond what is formally logged into the database as "engagement." At this early stage of the project, it is already clear that there are a range of definitions and perspectives on family engagement across and within the community schools. For instance, some stakeholder groups maintained a narrow definition of family engagement, viewing family involvement as limited to participation in school activities and receiving services. Others viewed family engagement more broadly, describing the potential for families and schools to work together in mutually beneficial partnerships to better support students. However, core strategies for engaging families seem to differ by school. These differences were influenced by each school's unique history and past relationships with families. In addition, each school has its own systems in place for communicating with and reaching out to families. For example, the process of recruiting parents for focus groups described earlier provided important insights into how schools functioned internally and how they interacted with parents.

Post-analysis action steps   When analyses are complete, the research team plans to meet with the director of school-community partnerships to share findings and create a dissemination plan. We will present findings to community school coordinators and principals and provide opportunities for districtwide and school-specific reflections on family engagement goals and strategies. At the outset of this qualitative study, the director established that findings from this work would be used to inform strategies for more effectively engaging families across the district. In addition, we expect that the findings will inform trainings for school-based staff.

CHALLENGES

Supplementing YDA data with survey or qualitative data proved to be important to the research, as well as to meeting practitioners' priorities and needs for actionable data. From our experience, administrative data do not speak as closely to practitioners' experiences as do qualitative data, and this observation is increasingly true the closer to the practice level a partner is. For example, when we discussed quantitative analyses of achievement test scores with teachers, they often wanted to know more about teaching practices or student engagement that is behind the scores, and these topics cannot be captured by administrative data. However, the benefits of supplemental data collection linked to administrative data analyses must be balanced with several unique challenges that are not present in using administrative data alone.

A primary issue is the amount of time and resources that qualitative or survey data collection take from practitioners and researchers, in comparison to analyses using administrative data. In both cases presented here, teachers and other school staff had to give up some of their time to help with data collection. Setting up the logistics of scheduling data collection can take a significant amount of time from both the research staff and the school or district staff. Because of time demands, it is important to think carefully about designing qualitative data collection or survey protocols as parsimoniously as possible. Also essential is creative thinking about the logistics of data collection to ensure minimal interruption of time for practitioners. Our work in meeting these goals and improving the process over time proved to be a key piece in responding to concerns about loss of instructional time. At the same time, several teachers wanted even more in-depth qualitative data on their specific practices in the classroom. Thus, logistics and buy-in complement each other: making logistics and time demands of data collection easy on practitioners helps gain buy-in from practitioners, while having practitioner buy-in opens the door for increasing the amount of time they are willing to devote to data collection.

Additionally, several of our partners have talked about "survey fatigue" due to many organizations and researchers wanting to collect data. This issue is particularly a concern for other organizations working in a university town, where there may be multiple researchers studying the same schools or youth. As a result, students are taking a lot of surveys, and we needed to be mindful of that fact. At the district's request, we worked with an organization administering an afterschool survey that asked students about some concepts that were similar to those in our middle school survey. We were able to develop a joint survey that combined both surveys with common items where appropriate, and we each used the data from the survey that students now only need to take once. An important reason that we were able to work on the joint survey is our long-standing partnership with RCSD.

In addition, there is an inherent problem in getting representative samples for research, particularly for interviews or focus groups that are connected to voluntary events that students, parents, or teachers choose to attend. This was less of an issue with the middle school survey because students were in the classes where the survey was administered, but it was a much larger issue with the family engagement study because it was harder to get access to the parents who did not typically participate in programs. We had originally hoped to use program participation data to identify these parents, but recruiting them proved to be problematic. Our success in gathering data from a representative group ultimately varied with each school depending on the communication structures that existed in any particular school. Having people on the JGC staff who could translate recruitment materials and conduct focus groups in Spanish was extremely important.

Another consideration is the extent to which we as the researchers directly collect data or build partners' capacity to collect data. From a research perspective, it is advantageous to ensure uniform administration of surveys by having our staff administer them rather than asking teachers to administer them. It also helps make students feel comfortable that their answers will remain confidential when they see that people from outside come to collect the surveys and take the surveys with them. Collecting surveys that we can link to individual students while maintaining student confidentiality requires a complex setup of using fictitious identification numbers that we can later link to students' real ID numbers, as described earlier. As researchers, we must adhere to strict guidelines of the Institutional Review Board, which oversees research at the university to ensure that research subjects' rights are protected, so it is difficult to delegate this responsibility to partners. At the same time, we would like to build schools' capacity to collect data so that the data collection does not rely solely on our involvement, but this has not yet happened because schools have limited resources, time, and expertise to devote to data collection.

Finally, there are challenges in sharing back findings. The more time we spend in direct contact with school staff, students, and families collecting data, the higher the expectations are that we share back results in ways meaningful to them. This means that the expectations for survey or qualitative data are often much higher than they are from analyses using only administrative data. However, confidentiality concerns are in some ways a much larger obligation with survey and qualitative data compared to administrative data. This comes into play with data reporting. For example, school principals frequently wanted to see findings presented for their own schools, but in qualitative research where a relatively small number of people are interviewed at each site, providing school-level data potentially risks the confidentiality of individuals' responses. Although partners found this disappointing, it is essential to our overall partnership to hold strict to confidentiality promises.

LESSONS LEARNED

One important lesson we have learned is that in order for research using qualitative or survey data to be accepted and used, it is vital to have strong buy-in from partners. This lesson is similar to those we have seen in other YDA work, but it is especially relevant when using qualitative or survey data because of the amount of time that community partners must spend either participating in or helping coordinate data collection. For the middle school survey, it took a long process of engaging partners and reframing our approach to have partners be fully invested and interested before they found the data useful enough to take action on it. Even though the idea originally came from partners, our process of engaging others in the district was critical. Over the three years that we have been conducting the survey, the dynamic has changed to a process that felt owned by the JGC to one that is owned by the district. The community school qualitative study had the advantage of being perceived as a response to what the partners wanted from the inception of the project. This perception was important because coordinating the data collection took a lot of the community school coordinators' time, and the data collection process would likely not have been as successful if the community school coordinators themselves had not been the ones asking the questions that led to the study.

Another lesson we have learned is the importance of being flexible in the research methodology. Reducing the length of the middle school survey was an important part of the process of making the survey more appealing to the schools. This decision to shorten the survey, however, was at the cost of breadth of theories and analyses that we could apply to our work with the schools. We may have lost an opportunity to learn about a wider range of practices or outcomes, but we gained buy-in from our partners, which was essential for the ongoing success of the research and to their acceptance of the findings. Requests to learn more and add breadth to the survey came later, and we were able to respond. Similarly, in both projects, we have found it important to give our partners a chance to weigh in on the research questions and data collection tools. Responding to these requests can take away from the rigor of the design but has been an important way to build partners' trust and perceived usefulness that ultimately make them more likely to utilize the findings. Our task is to maintain the integrity of the research and at the same time demonstrate our responsiveness to our partners' requests.

Engaging partners after analysis played an important role in ensuring action and ongoing research. Our partners on the middle school survey valued our outreach efforts, and their increased level of engagement over the course of the project has led to higher demand for the research as well as a greater likelihood that its results will prove actionable. An ongoing challenge with all of our research is translating and framing the work in a way that conveys the findings accurately and understandably so that the analysis is used as intended. Because the goal of the survey was not to evaluate, assess, or single out schools, teachers, or students, we are in a better position to learn together with practitioners in the district about practices that promote important learning attitudes and outcomes for students, especially for the highest-need students in the district.

NEXT STEPS

There are a number of directions that we would like to take these projects. Several follow-up questions have arisen that we cannot address with the survey data. Some schools have asked about using the survey data to evaluate particular schoolwide reforms, but answering those kinds of questions would require us to compare students who experienced a reform to those who did not, which is not possible because we cannot isolate the effects of a schoolwide reform from all of the other contextual factors within the school and in students' lives. Also, partners have expressed interest in extending the survey to older and younger grades to be able to examine how students fare in the transitions from elementary to middle school and middle to high school. For the family engagement study, even though the analysis is not complete, further questions that our partners are eager to understand are emerging. These include understanding the conditions necessary for families to become engaged and linking specific practices of family engagement programs to student outcomes.

At the same time, we are thinking about ways to sustain the survey data collection over time. Institutionalization of supplemental data collection would be ideal, but a method for automating the process so that it is not dependent on JGC researchers would help ensure that it happens. It is not yet clear what the method will be for doing this or if it is even desirable, given confidentiality issues. One possibility that the JGC is pursuing is developing an electronic survey application in partnership with the computer science department at Stanford that would allow us to come into classrooms with tablet computers that the students would use to take the survey. We are hopeful that this format of electronic surveying will make the process much more efficient and engaging for the students, but even this probably is not a strategy that schools can implement on their own.

Another way that we are hoping to institutionalize the survey is by broadening the partnership to include Sequoia High Union High School District (SUHSD), which is where most RCSD students go after eighth grade. We have begun administering a similar survey for the students at one SUHSD high school. Partners from both RCSD and the high school are excited about the possibility of being able to track data across the transition into high school, and the high school has an existing method of administering surveys online through their student information system. Perhaps the best road to institutionalization is having the data be included in routine reporting completed by schools or the school district.

8

WHAT MAKES THE YOUTH DATA ARCHIVE ACTIONABLE?

Kara Dukakis and Rebecca A. London

A fundamental premise of the Youth Data Archive is that its findings from cross-agency analyses should be useful to the involved partners in thinking about improvements or changes to youth policy or practice; in other words, that it be actionable. Providing actionable findings is a high standard for research, even community-engaged research, especially when it is not specifically focused on evaluating a program. It is therefore not surprising that one of the most difficult aspects of the initiative is to support partners in *using* the research findings, rather than just understanding and taking interest in them. Action can mean many things, however, and in this chapter we discuss definitions of action in the local environment, challenges to achieving action, and conditions that promote action, based on what we have gleaned from our work through the YDA.

DEFINING ACTION IN A LOCAL ENVIRONMENT

Literature on the definition of action in a local environment is sparse. As Nutley, Walter, and Davies state in their cross-sector examination of evidence-based practice, "Assessments of ways to encourage 'research use' usually don't define 'use.'"[1] Our definition of action draws from a few relevant and related fields of practice—data-driven decision making,[2] evidence-based practice,[3] and research use[4,5,6,7]—as well as from the small literature on multisector longitudinal administrative databases.[8,9] These fields tend to address similar issues and problems, and thus definitions of action overlap; for instance, the literature on integrated data systems emphasizes that a primary benefit of these systems is their ability to develop evidence-based policy.[10] The education literature focuses on data-driven decision making and defines the concept of actionable knowledge as the point at which decision makers synthesize data, prioritize goals, and consider and explore solutions.[11] Evidence-based practices are those that are substantiated by research; both this literature and the data-driven decision-making literature emphasize the importance of practitioner input in valuing, critiquing, and applying research[12] to use data to identify and clarify issues and problems, as well as to act on them. This process then becomes an iterative one as the action taken often generates a need for its own analysis.[13]

However, studies of research use go beyond stakeholder input to emphasize the process; as Tseng writes, "As important as getting the right people in the room is creating the conditions for back-and-forth discussions about the research and its implications."[14] The literature on integrated data systems also focuses on practitioner value and use and defines action as having four components: 1) capacity building to understand and translate analyses, 2) the resulting partnerships that develop among data-contributing organizations, 3) prioritization of public policy initiatives, and 4) leveraging resources across agencies.[15] As much of this literature focuses on state-level integrated data systems, the action tends to refer to policy changes or mandates at the state level.[16,17]

Drawing from these definitions and our experience, the YDA team defines action as taking many forms along a continuum: in our view, action can be any change in policy, practice, or programming; a determination to continue existing efforts; or even the *intention* to use research to discuss making changes or continuing with the status quo.[18] Such change may occur at the individual level (e.g., student or family), the setting level (e.g., school or classroom), or the system level (e.g., district, city or county, state). The continuum may be considered linear in that its ends are relatively concrete: one involves capacity building beginning at a very basic level; the other involves intentional and systematic use of research findings to make decisions in policy, practice, or programming. In between—and consistent with the definitions of action stated above—are capacity building and action at various levels, such as helping partners identify relevant researchable questions, critically review initial data outputs, comprehend analysis findings, translate or apply them in practice, and appreciate research as a means of improving outcomes. However, when applied, the continuum is much more nuanced, and components of action are rarely linear or mutually exclusive.

Intertwined with a continuum of action is the developmental arc of the YDA initiative itself and that of our relationship with each partner organization. Here, too, the relationship between the continuum and the developmental phase is not always linear: the developmental phase clearly influences what kind of action partners achieve, but additional factors (discussed later in the chapter) also contribute significantly.

Based on this definition, taking action is only possible, and the YDA initiative can only be successful, if community leaders believe in and are genuinely interested in engaging in a partnership with a research institution to explore data for the purpose of learning and positive change. In our experience, action stems from heavy engagement on the part of our community partners, before, during, and after the research is conducted. This engagement can be facilitated by having a formalized collaborative decision-making body act as the YDA "table" that engages with YDA researchers and guides the research and action processes. Finally, taking action is highly dependent on the developmental phase of the partnership between the community entity or collaborative and the research institution. As partnerships deepen, engagement does as well, and so we find that the length and extent of our relationship with partners is a fundamental factor in their willingness and ability to take action.

THE ROLE OF RESEARCH IN GENERATING ACTION

The role of research in generating community-led action is often depicted as challenging,[19] but when viewed as incremental changes on a continuum from capacity building to action in the context of deep partnership, the YDA brings a new perspective to this discussion. YDA analyses generate knowledge to inform community policies and practices, but explicitly do not make recommendations for specific actions. We assume that partners are the experts about the needs of their community and the feasibility of various options for addressing issues raised by YDA research. Instead, we have a seat at the collaborative table with the goal of explaining our analyses, building partner capacity to understand it, and providing support regarding options to improve practice and policy based on our research findings.

This approach distinguishes the YDA staff role from that of traditional evaluators, who are typically from organizations brought in to assess the effectiveness of a program or approach. It is important for evaluators to be objective analysts, meaning that they are neutral to the outcome of the research and not invested in the functioning of the program or approach in any way. The YDA researcher role is similarly neutral with regard to the content of the findings; we are invested in using the highest-quality research methods to generate findings on the research question at hand, and we are also objective and not invested in finding any particular issue or outcome. What distinguishes YDA staff from a typical external evaluation team is that we are not neutral with regard to the process; unlike traditional evaluators, we do not exit the setting once an analysis is finished, but are committed for the longer term. This stance allows not only work on identifying action with partners but also recursive analyses.

The YDA approach therefore supports a community-owned process throughout the life of any analysis or partnership—and we have increasingly encouraged partners to identify the action steps themselves, as opposed to preempting them with our own ideas about implications. We generally wait to finalize our written products until partners have had discussions of how they might use the new knowledge so that we may incorporate their ideas and plans into our publicly available issue briefs and other materials. For example, when presenting the YDA analysis of chronic absence in Redwood City, we were careful to share findings and some general implications (such as the need for an intentional system for collecting data required to conduct ongoing tracking of chronic absence), but little else on policy and action. This strategy fueled a robust discussion among partners, which generated ideas for action such as hiring an outside vendor to send letters to parents of chronically absent students.

Without exception, supporting partners to generate action from a YDA analysis has been the greatest obstacle to this work and is the aspect of the initiative that has taken the longest to develop. Following is a discussion of these challenges and their relationship to the actionability of research findings.

Action Requires Time, Resources, and Political Will

Despite what may be genuine enthusiasm and need on the front end of the YDA process, partners' lack of time, resources, and patience to make changes, especially during unprecedented budget shortfalls, can create delays and even roadblocks. Crises such as layoffs and cuts to basic services in addition to everyday pressures and a complicated political environment often take precedence over changes or improvements based on new analyses, however positive those improvements may be. Competing partner priorities also affect the YDA staff's ability to spend time on the application of research findings because partners must remain the primary drivers of the process in order for action to have meaning or "teeth." Competing partner priorities can also require that we work with partners to identify and develop cost-neutral policy approaches.

An additional related impediment to action is the high staff turnover in school districts, other public agencies, and community-based organizations, often due to budget cuts. Given that trust building and longevity of partnerships, along with partner capacity to understand research, are critical factors in the actionability of findings, frequent personnel shifts can mean time to reestablish not only trusting relationships but also partner appreciation of the value of the YDA and integrated longitudinal data analysis. In some cases, turnover also means loss of advocacy for involvement with the YDA, significantly slowing momentum.

ACTION BASED ON YDA ANALYSES CAN BE ELUSIVE

In many cases, action based on a YDA analysis does not occur immediately, or we are not present when it does take place. Sometimes we learn about changes to policy or practice later on, if at all. For example, several years after completion of an analysis of physical fitness and academic achievement (chapter 3), we learned that the district superintendent incorporated physical activity as a strategy to increase student achievement in the district's plan and in the schools' individual site plans, and also used these findings to help obtain a grant from the local health-care district to support more physical education programming. Three years after completing the foster youth and education analysis (chapter 4), we learned that advocates have used the report to help shape state legislation. Complicating this picture, funders tend to support short-term projects that may allow for the first step toward action, whereas the true effects or outcomes often are not apparent for a significant period of time afterwards.

Analysis Time Can Extend the Action Time Frame

The time involved in conducting a YDA analysis itself can delay opportunities to take action because of the highly sensitive individually identifiable data we use and the importance of establishing deep, trusting relationships with partners. Potential partners are often initially hesitant to share highly sensitive data with us. This caution can require YDA staff to provide multiple verbal assurances outlined in our data use agreements (see appendixes 2 and 3) and proof of concept based on previous analyses with other partners. Once we embark on an analysis, our reliance on regular partner feedback to preliminary findings adds time. The final steps of the YDA analysis can also create a lag; we stand by our practice of fully vetting each analysis with every data-contributing agency, but this principle frequently challenges agency directors to find the time to carefully review final written products prior to their dissemination. The YDA analysis process itself, therefore, can delay partners' ability to take action based on findings.

Keeping partners engaged in the research for the amount of time it takes to complete it elongates the process, but sometimes the policy window in which to act is more immediate. In these cases, we attempt to provide preliminary documents that partners can use in order to continue in their process, but still complete the full and formal analysis so that any action can be substantiated with rigorous research. While our past experience demonstrates that it often took partners time—occasionally even years—to act on analysis findings, more recently they have responded to our lengthy analysis and deliverables process by making changes based on our presentations of early findings, showing their eagerness (or need) to move toward positive change as quickly as possible. A more rapid findings-to-action response may also owe to the fact that several analyses for the same partners build upon one another over time, honing in on the policies or programs requiring action and enabling a more targeted approach to taking action. And finally, a quick-action response clearly reflects a higher level of trust in us by partners as well as the YDA staff's increasing ability to be flexible in responding to partners' needs.

Collaborative or Multisector Action Can Be Complicated

Collaborative action—one of the primary goals of YDA—may be relatively easy to discuss in theory, but shared responsibility for taking action brings collaboration to a new level beyond collaborative research. In our work, and at the far and most mature end of the action continuum, shared responsibility for taking action involves explicit commitments from partners to amend existing policy or practice or develop new policy or practice based on findings, along with accountability for follow-through. Because YDA analyses are cross-cutting, commitments to take action are often dispersed between or among the involved agencies, and they sometimes require joint development of new policies or programs. Partners may hesitate to make such a commitment because, either directly or by implication, taking action may be an admission that their agency's status-quo policy is not effective, or worse, contributes to negative outcomes. For example, when partners discussed findings from our analysis of the educational outcomes of foster youth, they asked whether the educational needs of youth in the child welfare system were the job of the school district or of the human services agency. The answer was both, and the expected obstacle lay in dividing specific tasks between the two agencies and to different levels within each. In this case, the intermediary advocacy organization that had originally convened the group worked with both agencies to create action.

CONDITIONS THAT PROMOTE ACTIONABLE FINDINGS

The following section describes the conditions that we find affect actionability. As we detailed earlier, ownership of the work is shared between the YDA staff and community partners; for this reason, we have included both the YDA researcher perspective and the partner perspective whenever possible in describing critical conditions for action. Because partnerships deepen and evolve over time (and as such influence action), actionability is situated in the context of the specific developmental phase of the YDA–community entity partnership and in the phase of the YDA initiative itself. Not all of our analyses resulted in action as defined by programmatic or policy change or development, but all have resulted in action along the broad capacity-building-to-action continuum described previously. The facilitating conditions we present here, the challenges we previously described, and the developmental phase of the YDA initiative and partnerships all play a part in how and when partners take action along the continuum.

The Role of Deep Partnerships with the Community

The longer YDA staff are involved with a group of agencies in a community, the more we understand and appreciate the nature and value of their work and its context. A deeper understanding of partners' work and context enables us to produce responsive, relevant, and meaningful analyses, which increases the likelihood that partners will use the findings to inform action.

YDA partners have a broad range of experiences and resulting capacity to understand, interpret, and use data. These differences clearly play a role in their ability to take action. However, it is evident that partners' willingness to engage in action relates to growing trust in YDA researchers as they witness the quality of our work and our commitment to work alongside them. The result of increased partner trust can manifest differently at different points in our relationship with them. When, based on a history of relationship and trust building, partners invite YDA staff to participate as the data arm for an existing initiative, it often means that a collaborative group with a purpose and goals has already been formed and is ready for cross-agency data analysis that will help push the work forward. Thereafter, when the same partners embed the YDA as the research and data component into an existing initiative, or at least a collaborative of agency and organizational representatives, it creates a more organic process. Over time, YDA staff can become an invaluable part—and sometimes close to a permanent fixture—of the group, relied upon not only for the analyses themselves but also for information on evidence-based interventions or critical updated information and data related to the topic at hand.

An example of how the trust between partner and YDA staff can lead to action over time occurred with our chronic absence analysis in Redwood City (chapter 4). Although we had not previously conducted an analysis specifically at the request of the collaborative body Redwood City 2020 (RWC 2020), we had previously conducted at least one analysis for each of the data-contributing partners and were a known, trusted entity. This history and trust directly affected the YDA staff's seamless work with the collaborative and frequent presence at their meetings to discuss steps in the chronic absence analysis and findings.

The Organizational Level of YDA Partnerships

The organizational level at which the YDA relationship is formed is another critical factor in the ultimate generation of action in response to findings. YDA partners generally include individuals at the executive, middle management, data gatekeeper, and administrative levels. At times, action occurs more easily when the leaders of an initiative intentionally convene partners at different organizational levels or in different roles into committees or working groups with specific charges and responsibilities.

Partners' intentional creation of such a structure is generally a sign of their high capacity to move from research findings to action, and to a more advanced relationship with YDA staff.

Such has been the case with San Francisco's Bridge to Success initiative (BtS), which employs an infrastructure of cross-agency working groups focused on different relevant topics, largely made up of practitioners (see chapters 2 and 5). BtS also includes a steering committee, made up of middle managers and some agency directors, which acts as the "spine" of the initiative, and an executive committee, made up of high-level administrators like the school district superintendent and community college chancellor, which reacts to analysis findings with proposals for large-scale systemic reform intended to improve student outcomes. YDA researchers participate in all levels of this infrastructure, which is both sophisticated and effective as a lever for creating policy and programmatic action.

The Generation of New Relationships Out of Prior YDA-Partner Relationships

The formation of YDA relationships with partners can take months and in some cases even years, but even an informally established connection at one point in time with a particular community partner can lead to or support more formal partnerships in the future. This component is critical in the developmental arc of both our relationship with partners and the YDA initiative's growth over time.

In Redwood City, our long-standing community schools work with the RWC 2020 collaborative prompted their request for new analyses of two related initiatives—the Sequoia Teen Resource Center at a district high school, and the San Mateo County (Alcohol and Other Drug) Prevention Partnership. Partners saw the value of our YDA community schools work and wanted to be able to replicate the two main aspects of it for other analyses: namely, the consolidation of various programs and services into distinct but logical categories, and the subsequent linking of service participation data on individual youth to school outcome data. In the course of this subsequent work, partners also saw the need for alignment of analyses focused on programs that serve the same youth. They requested inclusion of common youth development indicators of success across initiatives, which has resulted in additional data collections with improved and more uniform measures, ultimately enhancing the quality of the research.

The Need for YDA Work to Be Driven from the Outset by Partners

YDA researchers intentionally engage partners from the beginning and throughout the analysis, sharing back findings frequently, soliciting feedback and updates on relevant issues that arise, incorporating their suggestions for additional analysis pieces, and securing their approval and input on final written products. Moving from data to action requires partners to make a clear time and resource investment from the outset, designating specific staff to be involved in the analysis. They must make a commitment to collaborate with the other partners at the table to both understand the research and to use it to reach mutually agreeable solutions that will improve outcomes for the youth they collectively serve. Although YDA researchers make every effort to minimize the burdens placed on partners, their ongoing involvement and leadership is essential to the actionability of findings.

With early partner engagement, we can ensure that YDA analyses focus on pressing community needs. As described in chapter 1, this includes joint development very early on of research questions and initial "fact sheets" or policy analyses that help community partners dig deeper into their questions and data. These early products serve to provide interim feedback and findings to keep partners engaged, but also offer a point to reassess the research questions in order to make sure they respond to important community questions. Early involvement also helps to support action during the entire course of the research project, including capacity building for improving the quality of data collection as well as for understanding and ultimately broader dissemination of findings.

The Use of Funding to Support Actionable Research

The notions of partners having "skin in the game," coupled with accountability to an outside funder, have proven to be critical to promoting action. The study of foster youth and education (chapter 4) was our first experience in which a partner directly tied a request for an analysis to funding. In this case, a local community foundation provided financial support while partnering with a local foster youth advocacy organization that convened many of the stakeholders in the foster care and juvenile justice fields, facilitated meetings, and ultimately pushed action forward. The funds came from an individual donor of the community foundation, which presented a new opportunity for the work because the funder participated in meetings and in the JGC's presentation of findings. This combination of funding, infrastructure (in the form of a table of stakeholders brought together by the lead agency with some support from the JGC), and advocacy proved highly effective. Our interactions with both the main group and a smaller group of involved partners were focused and productive. The lead agency took the initiative to develop committees of the larger group, and charged one of these with disseminating research findings and catalyzing improvements in practice at the district and school levels focused on foster youth. The director of the lead agency and the funding partner also presented the research findings at multiple school board meetings and events, urging members to improve their policies with regard to foster youth. Finally, our strong partnership with both the funder and the advocacy group provided the credibility we needed to present our findings to the foster care community.

The Role of Advocacy Organizations in Moving Findings to Action

The JGC is not an advocacy organization and does not make recommendations or promote specific practices or policies based on the research findings. But advocacy groups can have important connections to decision makers and are uniquely positioned to influence them. Though we have not partnered with advocacy organizations to use our research to initiate or further a cause, we and our partners have been struck by the efficacy of this strategy.

Again, the BtS initiative provides a strong example, as it included among its many partners the largest advocacy organization for children and youth in San Francisco. This agency, in collaboration with a student-led group from the community college, used the YDA findings to wage a campaign to significantly reform the college placement process. The advocacy group held a rally, produced flyers, generated a petition that collected more than eight hundred signatures, and testified at a number of community college board hearings. Although it is impossible to assess their effectiveness apart from the broader effort, we believe that they activated a large and vocal constituency which pushed decision makers toward meaningful action. Use of data by advocacy groups, accurately or not, is an inherent risk of producing and disseminating research, particularly when public sector institutions are involved, but can vastly increase the potential for positive action.[20]

Youth-Centered Data Discussions Among Stakeholders as a Means of Promoting Cross-Agency Collaboration and Action

YDA researchers regularly stress and reinforce the importance of focusing on the broad shared goal of improving youth outcomes across agencies as a key YDA premise. Ultimately, the ability to embrace this approach and enter into collaborative data-driven decision making depends on partners' willingness to put aside independent agendas (and related defenses) and join together in a "youth sector" that shares responsibility for the well-being of children and youth across multiple domains. Once this shift occurs, appropriate parties may take on specific follow-up actions, but with an ongoing commitment to remain collaborative in the process of reform.

Nearly all YDA analyses promote the youth sector approach. However, its benefit is most apparent where partners simultaneously or sequentially serve the same sets of youth without having an opportunity to see how these young people succeed in other domains. This first look across settings was illuminating for partners in all YDA analyses. But to move from illuminating issues and opportunities to action requires the additional conditions discussed in this chapter.

CONCLUDING THOUGHTS

In this chapter we defined action along a broad continuum ranging from building the capacity to use data and research to broad-scale educational reform. Action points along the continuum are not mutually exclusive in that we often provide ongoing capacity building for partners to understand findings while they are brainstorming ways to act on them. Capacity building is not always a prerequisite for policy-based action; in some cases, partners were poised to take action at the beginning of our formal partnership with them. Similarly, the relationship between the continuum of action and the developmental phase of the YDA and our relationship with partners is linear in some cases but not at all in others. At times, the longer our relationship with partners and the more mature the initiative, the more actionable the findings were, but this was not true in every experience; again, other facilitating (or constraining) conditions played a role.

Along with the growth of the YDA initiative, our staff has gained significant insight into the factors that affect partners' ability and willingness to take action, and we have adjusted our process accordingly. We will continue to feed insights into our YDA process and understanding of the action continuum to make the analyses as effective and informative as possible to immediate partners as well as the growing field of integrated longitudinal data systems.

9

THE YOUTH DATA ARCHIVE IN REFLECTION

Contributions to the Local Youth Sector and Research Community

Rebecca A. London and Milbrey McLaughlin

As described in chapter 1, the Youth Data Archive operates through a mutually beneficial university-community partnership between researchers at the Gardner Center at Stanford University and participating community agencies and stakeholders. These include elementary, secondary, and postsecondary school districts, county and city agencies, and youth-serving nonprofit organizations. Agencies that participate in the YDA agree to share their individual-level data with each other and the JGC for research purposes in order to ask and answer questions about youth that they otherwise would be unable to examine. The YDA's primary goals are to support community efforts to improve youth services and outcomes, advance interagency collaboration, and contribute to the larger field of youth-focused research.

The YDA takes a "youth sector" perspective, recognizing that a multitude of agencies and organizations serve youth within the community to meet their academic, social, emotional, and physical development needs. It bridges across so-called institutional silos to conduct cross-agency research that can support collaboration among youth-serving agencies and a broad community perspective on youth-serving investments. In this way, the collaboration and shared agenda fostered by YDA analyses promote joint responsibility and accountability for youth outcomes. We have intentionally shaped the YDA process to center on our partnerships with community organizations and have built in several features to support partners' interest and willingness to share their confidential data. The JGC is a neutral third party at the collaborative research table, holding data for the benefit of the community as a whole rather than for any particular agency. We stand by the principle that the community owns the data and must approve any use of data as well as any release of findings. We take a user-focused approach to the research; the research topics and questions that drive the analyses respond to needs identified by partners. Finally, we make a long-term commitment to our community partners, which is essential in building the trusting relationships needed to engage in this work. Together, these features support an iterative research process that is the backbone of the capacity-building-to-action continuum discussed in chapter 8.

THE YDA AS A RESOURCE FOR STRENGTHENING PARTNERS' CAPACITY AND THE LOCAL YOUTH SECTOR

YDA analyses provide community partners with new information about each other's work in the local youth sector, details about the experiences and pathways of the youth they serve, and data with which to advocate for their particular goals or for the wider needs of the community's youth. YDA analyses are often the first chance partners have to see individually linked, cross-agency data and to look across institutional boundaries to consider youth policies and practices in broader, more collective terms. Partners agree that YDA analyses are valuable for the cross-institutional perspectives they inform. But the YDA's contributions to partners and community youth development extend beyond this discrete analytical work. The YDA's process and supports serve as a resource and catalyst both for strengthening community partners' own capacity to use and understand research and for building the local youth sector more generally.

Building Partners' Capacity

Expanding and improving data collection   It has been an important learning experience for partners that the analyses the YDA can provide are only as good as the data that populate their systems. Seeing the limitations of what they can learn from their own data through the YDA has spurred some partners to expand and improve their data collection systems. It is not uncommon for YDA researchers to encounter instances of missing or incorrect data in an analysis, realities that diminish the power of YDA findings. Some problems are the result of inadequate data entry or collection strategies; others are due to data that has not previously been collected but that YDA analyses have shown are important to answering pressing questions. As a result of YDA research, for instance, the Redwood City School District initiated a new data collection system to capture student and family participation in its community school programs. The system has allowed for complex analyses of these schools that have made the research in Redwood City a national model in this field.

From partners' perspectives, data shortcomings have also resulted from the nature of administrative data. As discussed in chapter 7, substantive limitations of administrative data have prompted some partners to request or initiate research using other methods—surveys, focus groups, and interviews—in order to better understand the processes at work that link service provision to student outcomes. These primary data collections are extremely valuable for supplementing existing agency data.

Supporting ongoing learning opportunities   YDA involvement strengthens partners' capacity to learn about youth's needs and identify resources available to address them. Again, the community schools analysis offers an example. At the practitioner level, YDA researchers led "data talks" with school-level staff involved with this analysis to deepen their understanding of the factors affecting student and parent experiences in the community schools and the outcomes associated with them. These data talks offered an important opportunity for principals, teachers, and other staff to gain a more sophisticated understanding of the elements important to the effective functioning of a community school and about the research questions they could pose for a next round of analyses. They used the information to think about their everyday practices and whether the findings aligned with their own views of how community schools were functioning. We are starting to use the data talk strategy in other YDA projects as a strategy to promote partners' learning about data interpretation and implications for action. In reporting back to agency leaders and collaborative bodies, we typically spend time going into greater detail about the analysis methods and findings, which partners need to approve before dissemination can occur. Partners typically ask many questions and often request clarifying information or other future analyses to help them think about how to respond. These are key opportunities for capacity building because helping partners to understand complex research analyses deepens their understanding of and appreciation for the research as well as their appetite for future research projects.

The iterative research process embodied by the YDA provides ample opportunities for using capacity building to fuel future research, but there is a downside to this approach as well. It can be difficult to know when a particular topic of study is complete because partners may become so invested in the work that they want to continue to analyze data long after funds for the project and the timeline laid out have expired. This challenge is, in some ways, the best kind to have because it speaks to the investment of partners in the process.

Strengthening the Local Youth Sector

Increased coherence of policy and practice Discussions among community partners about data and about implications prompted by YDA analyses can increase the coherence of the various institutional policies and practices affecting local youth. In some cases, research showing misalignment between two systems has prompted action, as was the case in the alternative education analysis (chapter 2), the foster care analysis (chapter 4), and the Bridge to Success work (chapters 2 and 5). Partners have talked about the utility of the YDA approach in helping them quell tensions among their colleagues by demonstrating the reality that "these are all our kids," even if each agency serves them in different ways. The YDA also supports coherence by reducing the finger-pointing that comes from territoriality and defensiveness of a siloed approach to youth policy making. Being on the same team, so to speak, helps create productive collaborative efforts, even among organizations that might normally compete for scarce resources.

Building and maintaining partnerships Deep partnerships are essential to the success of the YDA and underlie a strong youth sector approach to community youth development. The YDA has motivated new partnerships among youth-serving agencies and deepened and strengthened existing collaborative efforts. For instance, the chronic absence research that was conducted in collaboration with Redwood City 2020 has extended the engagement between the health and education sectors in new ways. The Bridge to Success analyses provided substantial material for collaborative working groups, made up of secondary and postsecondary stakeholders, to ponder and discuss. In these instances and others, the YDA has been able to demonstrate to community partners that their work is part of a broader effort that requires, and would benefit from, the participation of other youth-serving organizations in order to align goals and provide a streamlined set of services to youth and their families.

A central frustration to these deepening relationships, both among the partners themselves and between the partners and the YDA, is the institutional churn associated with new leadership, retirements, or staff reductions at partner agencies. This turnover complicates YDA operations and can undermine established understandings and commitment to the YDA collaborative. This institutional reality makes it important to ensure buy-in at multiple organizational levels, including at the director level, with the data managers, and with other middle managers who have the ability to push forward or stall YDA activities.

THE LOCAL ADVANTAGE

"Local advantage" refers to the particular opportunities community partners have for action given their local knowledge of resources, multiple professional and personal connections, interlocking loyalties and networks, and flexibility in making changes to policy and practice. Local actors occupy an advantaged position in their ability to diagnose problems and potential to pursue cross-agency solutions. Unlike the partisan politics that often fracture policy debates and action at state and national levels, community partners at the local level can transcend such divisiveness to unite around a common focus and responsibility for the community's youth. YDA's community partners understand issues related to the youth they serve in up-close, personal terms, rather than as disembodied statistics or decontextualized accounts provided by state or national reports. The YDA plays to partners' local advantage by providing them the data that allow them to speak in more than generalities about concerns that implicate multiple youth-serving agencies and to draw upon established relationships, familiar positions, and deep local knowledge to consider new, cross-agency responses.

Further, community partners are advantaged by their ability to act quickly compared to actors at state or national levels, and can create new policies and practices one step at a time, rather than await formal shifts in regulatory language or institutional procedures as is often required for change at other levels of government. Community leaders can act strategically and make adaptations to existing policies and practices—as with the City College of San Francisco's decision to change their placement policies—or initiate new ones—as with the expansion of the community school strategy within the Redwood City School District—on their own authority.

The YDA also supports the local advantage by enabling local actors and their communities to locate national trends and concerns in terms of the issues and opportunities that affect "their kids" and then develop situation-specific responses. The Foster and Delinquent Youth Education Data Working Group stressed the importance of having local data, for instance, to be able to advocate for policy and programmatic improvements for their youth. Although the problem of students' low rate of community college graduation has received national attention, it was not until the Bridge to Success analyses showed how San Francisco Unified graduates fared at the City College of San Francisco that concrete action was taken. The YDA analysis of chronic absenteeism in the elementary and high school district likewise permitted community partners to frame the issue in terms of local demographics, challenges, and supports, and to issue a call to action in the form of RCSD's outreach to kindergarten parents.

LAUNCHING AND SUSTAINING A YOUTH DATA ARCHIVE

As discussed in chapter 6, initial YDA partnerships can take time to develop. In the very first analyses, beginning in 2005, partners were skeptical about the value of the project, the motives of the researchers, and the potential for findings to be used in ways that could shed unfavorable light on their organizations. Without a demonstration of the value of the project to show partners how the cross-agency approach to research could benefit them—and more importantly, the youth they serve—it was difficult to convince them to share their confidential data through the YDA. We learned with these initial organizations some fundamental lessons about how to do this work with maximum benefit to, and minimal burden on, the partners themselves.

We relied in the beginning on our strong ties with community organizations in Redwood City to demonstrate the value of the YDA project. Our history with the elementary school district was vital because school district data are core to the YDA. The district holds information on the population of youth in the community. With the exceptions of children who are not yet of school age and those who attend private school, school district data capture information on all children and youth and therefore provide the base from which data matching occurs. The school district is also essential because academic achievement is one of the major youth outcome areas that concern communities—and these data are collected most accurately and consistently by educational institutions themselves. From district data, matches can be made to a variety of other organizations to understand how their services interact, who accesses them (and who does not), and whether and how services play a role in helping students progress in school. Ideally, matches would be made to a variety of external partners providing services in the same sector (e.g., health or afterschool) to provide an even broader understanding of access to and uptake of services.

As with any new endeavor, a principal challenge is that in order to attract funders one needs to show proof of concept, but without funds, conducting the necessary research is not possible. Especially at the onset of the YDA initiative, when its utility was uncharted, agencies were reluctant to share their limited financial and human capital resources to prioritize data extraction and transfer for the YDA. Financial resources for conducting research and reporting findings, as well as for partnership and capacity building, were similarly limited, a reality which frustrated collaboration and limited attention to YDA needs and activities. Initial YDA analyses relied on external funds secured by the Gardner Center to support general operations rather than funds targeted to support the YDA itself or a particular analysis. Over time, and as partners began to see the value of the work, we moved from this strategy toward one in which partners themselves invested in the analyses, either through their own funds or through externally secured grants with a research component. Financial investment in the process has improved partner commitment to the process and to use of the findings to support changes in policy or practice on the ground. When partners contribute funding to support the analysis, the topic areas and research questions that form are closely tied to their work and support the iterative research process. An investment in the work can lead them to ask more detailed questions, which in turn affords YDA staff the opportunity to provide capacity building not only in understanding research findings but also in using findings to think critically about future work.

As partners become invested in the YDA and see its benefit for their work, their commitment to the process facilitates a shift in norms and values toward fostering a community of practice across sectors. Critical to this shift is that the analyses be not merely interesting research pieces but needed and useful tools so that partners can respond collectively to the findings. Over time, as our partnerships in Redwood City have developed and deepened, and as we have expanded YDA work in the Bay Area, we find that financial investment coupled with a forum for cross-agency collaboration are indispensable conditions for supporting the actionability of the findings.

How to direct partners toward this goal of shared question formation itself presents a challenge. Bringing partners together simply to discuss what the YDA might do for them—a strategy we tried early on—was not productive. Without urgency about a problem and community interest in the findings, it is unlikely that the research will be actionable. One partner gave an important piece of advice: find opportunities for inserting yourself into existing collaborative meetings and work through those groups to identify research questions. We took this advice and embedded our researchers into ongoing community meetings. This strategy has been useful both for identifying topics of interest and also for being recognized as a resource to help community partners think about data and research.

Still, these collaborative meetings are not always or regularly attended by director-level agency staff, whose buy-in is needed for the YDA's operation and actionability. Multilevel strategies are needed to ensure that YDA staff stay apprised of the research areas that partners are grappling with, and that analyses respond to the policy and practice questions that are most needed. Toward that end, the JGC executive director and associate director also frequently attend meetings with agency leaders on a variety of topics. As we become better known in the communities in which we work, word of mouth and personal referrals, as well as continued analyses for the same set of partners, have taken hold as the primary means for identifying research opportunities.

HOW YDA RESEARCH DIFFERS FROM TRADITIONAL UNIVERSITY-BASED RESEARCH

By design, the YDA's approach to research differs from the approach traditionally employed by many university-based researchers. Academic institutions tend to reward scholarship that meets a discipline-defined standard of excellence, which rarely, if ever, includes on-the-ground action as a criterion. Indeed, since the 1970s observers have been keenly aware that research findings rarely make their way outside of academia and into the hands of decision makers, especially at the local level, even when the goal is change in policy or practice. Community partners' perception of research as an ivory-tower undertaking initially slowed the growth of the YDA, as we struggled to assure partners that we would not use their data to conduct research that was irrelevant to their everyday practice. The problem of research non-use has been identified and discussed largely from the researcher side, focusing on how research can be differently conceived, conducted, and presented to enhance its use by policy makers and practitioners. In contrast, the YDA's approach focuses on the decision-maker or user side of the process, going to considerable lengths to ensure that the voice of community partners is present in all aspects of the work—from inquiry to design to action.

The YDA process represents a fundamental shift in how rigorous research is conceived and conducted, and this stance brings significant benefits to the initiative along with substantial challenges. The benefits have been detailed throughout this book with examples of the many ways our partners have engaged with the YDA and used findings to promote changes in their communities to better address youth's needs. The frustrations are also many, and we find ourselves treading in uncharted territory as we stay close to the principles of the YDA process while also attending as much as possible to the standards of academic scholarship. We struggle continually with the question of how to conduct YDA research that meets the academy's standards of quality on the one hand and, on the other, users' need for research that is relevant and valid in their terms, timely, and readily applicable to local problems.

For example, research questions and topics that our partners value are not always the ones that inform the literature in meaningful ways, a feature valued by academic scholarship. In many cases, partners' organizational and political contexts for action require them to replicate on the local level findings from a national- or state-level study in order to motivate community-level response. Replication research of this sort is enormously useful to partners but does not always advance the field-building mission of the YDA because it does not extend or elaborate existing research-based literature.

In addition, it is sometimes difficult to balance our neutrality as researchers with our role as engaged community partners. Community partners sometimes would like to see us undertaking more evaluative research focused on identifying the impact of a particular program or set of programs. We veer away from such evaluative work as compromising our ability to serve as an impartial partner dedicated to building capacity within the broad youth sector. Rather than be detached from our partners with our research as evaluators typically are, we attempt to be active partners in their work so that cross-agency research and analysis becomes the way that they approach questions related to youth policy and practice in their community.

A third challenge is in presenting findings to partners in ways that are useful and understandable to them. As has been described in previous chapters, analyses undertaken with the YDA typically use complex statistical methods that generate findings in forms that partners find confusing and not helpful. It is incumbent upon the researchers to report these findings in ways that make sense and are useful to community partners. However, reporting can also be difficult when the metrics approved as best practice in the academic literature are different from the metrics that decision makers use in their work. An example is the California Standards Test (CST) results. CST results are reported by the California Department of Education (CDE) as scale scores up to 600, and are also converted into a five-point scale of proficiency from far below basic to advanced for each subject area. The CDE is clear that the scale scores are not comparable across grades or years, meaning that it is not appropriate to compare a student's fourth-grade math scale score to her fifth-grade score and assess progress based on the comparison. One can compare progress by looking at the five-point scale of proficiency, but improvements in student performance can be masked by these broad categories. The literature tends to use the scale scores, but converts them to a "z-score," which is a way of normalizing the scale scores so that they can be compared across grades and years. However, partners are unsure how to use analyses that report z-scores because this is a metric they do not consider. They prefer the five-point proficiency scale, which is more in accord with their practice, but less precise for research purposes.

As described in chapter 7, on-the-ground research requires adjustments to the standard definitions of validity and reliability in survey research. From the academic perspective, the most valid and reliable instruments are those that have been tested by prior research. However, in conforming to those standards, we were unable either to respond to partners' concerns about how the findings would be received (and consequently used) or to address the context-specific questions that partners were hoping to answer. In this case, altering the exact language of the survey questions served to improve local validity but ruled out comparisons to the broader literature on those modified questions.

CONCLUDING THOUGHTS

The YDA has provided an opportunity to witness firsthand the progress that can occur in local communities when cross-agency data are infused into decision-making processes. Chapter 8 lays out a continuum of action from capacity building to policy change, identifying the multiple ways that the engaged research of the YDA can influence community policies and processes. We take this continuum a bit farther to show that actionability itself is part of the feedback cycle, as depicted in figure 9.1.

The YDA's iterative process of research and focus on users promotes capacity building among partners both to understand and use research, and also to collaborate with each other in building a local youth sector. Actions that result from this work strengthen the bonds of the youth sector, which in turn enhance its ability to promote positive change on behalf of youth in the local context.

This iterative process also is fundamental to the sustainability of the Youth Data Archive; as research projects prompt on-the-ground action, there is a new opportunity to inform local practice by understanding how changes in the local youth sector continue to affect resources, opportunities, and outcomes for youth. We are now moving into that territory and in the upcoming years will be tracking the ways that Redwood City's approach to combating chronic absence changes students' attendance patterns (chapter

Figure 9.1 Using capacity and action to strengthen the youth sector: a cyclical process

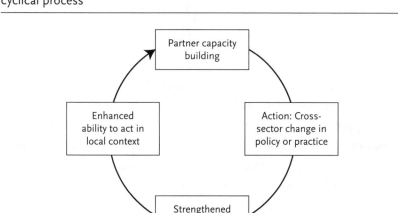

4), as well as the ways that City College of San Francisco's new remediation pilot programs change course-taking and success among new students (chapters 2 and 5). It is clear that the long-term commitment to community, trust building, capacity building, and iterative research process were fundamental to reaching this point in the actionability feedback cycle.

We will continue to engage in collaborative research with our valued Bay Area partners. There are many more questions to answer and multiple opportunities for new research trajectories. As always, funding remains a central challenge that limits the number of projects we can undertake simultaneously. With many demonstrations of YDA's value in hand, we are hopeful that funders will recognize the benefit of this approach to research and begin to fund not only the individual projects that make up the YDA, but the broader approach to building a youth sector.

With seven years of research behind us, our work is becoming known beyond our partner communities. Expanding to new Bay Area or more distant communities is another burgeoning sustainability strategy. Indeed, we are beginning a partnership with a southern California community that serves a large number of public school students. We are testing the approach of a long-distance relationship by starting with just one contributing partner (the school district) and then building relationships with other local partners through initial research questions focused on college readiness.

The Youth Data Archive model, and others that similarly rely on university-community research partnerships, push the current notions of scholarship in ways that can be uncomfortable to academic institutions and researchers within them. However, we have compelling examples of how engaged scholarship that employs rigorous research strategies and responds to community-identified needs to motivate action is field-building work. Building a youth sector has been, and will hopefully continue to be, recognized by the community and the academy as advancing the field of youth development in new and critical ways.

LEGAL GUIDELINES FOR DATA SHARING AND CONFIDENTIALITY

DATA SHARING AND CONFIDENTIALITY

Youth Data Archive (YDA) analyses rely entirely on individually identifiable data on youth, including name, date of birth, address, and occasionally social security number. Beyond this, depending on the organization contributing data, Gardner Center (JGC) staff receive information attached to each individual that may include school outcomes (grades, standardized test scores, attendance, behavior, credits accrued); child welfare experiences (case status, placement type, placement location, number of placements over time, reunification attempts and services received); afterschool, recreational, or violence prevention program participation; and dosage, mental health diagnosis, and services received, among other items. Storing and analyzing individually identified data by these categories requires attention to the highly sensitive nature of the information, and the JGC is required to comply with all relevant laws and regulations for data security, privacy, and confidentiality.

The JGC is able to acquire and work with such highly sensitive data because YDA analyses only report data in aggregated form and because the data are used for research purposes by a recognized research institution.

Different laws or parts of laws govern case management lookup systems from those that govern systems linking administrative data sets for research purposes.

Beyond legal and regulatory limits, the JGC has elected to provide YDA partners with a high degree of control over the process; the data remain theirs regardless of how they are combined, analyzed, written up, or disseminated. This policy reflects the JGC's deeply held principle of working in partnership with organizations. The means by which the JGC codifies these pledges and stipulations is through a data use agreement (DUA; see appendixes 2 and 3 for samples), similar to a memorandum of understanding but specific to the storage and security of data.

All YDA data are stored on a secure server managed by Stanford's Information Technology Services (ITS) division. The server is not connected to the Internet and has secured entry and 24-hour monitoring. Stanford ITS has created a written data security protocol (provided in appendix 4), and we have established introductory training measures for new staff, including directions for uploading data, and a required course of data security training sessions offered by the University. After completing their training they are given a certificate indicating that they have carefully reviewed the data security protocols and they understand the potential negative consequences of releasing confidential data.

FEDERAL AND STATE REGULATIONS REGARDING INDIVIDUALLY- IDENTIFIABLE DATA

Following are the primary federal and California state regulations governing the use and disclosure of education, health, and child welfare data that are individually identifiable. In general, these require both a data use and disclosure agreement between or among the involved parties and a data security protocol that defines how the entity receiving the data will provide for its storage and security. Overall, these regulations attempt to strike a balance between protecting personal information and allowing the use of information for inquiry or policy. Limits are placed on research institutions for conducting research and sharing data on individual youth.

Federal Regulations

Federal Privacy Act of 1974[1]   The federal Privacy Act of 1974 (5 U.S.C. § 552a) establishes a code of fair information practices that governs the collection, maintenance, use, and dissemination of any kind of information or data about individuals that is maintained in systems of records by federal agencies. The Privacy Act prohibits the disclosure of a record about an individual from a system of records without the written consent of the individual, unless the disclosure is pursuant to one of twelve statutory exceptions. The relevant exception for the YDA states that the disclosure be "to a recipient who has provided the agency with advance adequate written assurance that the record will be used solely as a statistical research or reporting record, and the record is to be transferred in a form that is not individually identifiable."[2] This suggests encryption of the data file during transfer. While the Privacy Act does not directly apply to the YDA because it specifically covers federal agencies, it is widely cited in as a key guideline for disclosing individually identifiable data.

Family Educational Rights and Privacy Act of 1974 (FERPA)[3]   The Family Educational Rights and Privacy Act (20 U.S.C. § 1232g; 34 CFR) is a federal law that protects the privacy of education records, affording parents the right to have access to their children's education records,[4] the right to seek to have the records amended, and the right to consent to the disclosure of personally identifiable information from education records, except as provided by law.

The law also includes exceptions to confidentiality and prior consent to release of educational records; a number of these exceptions apply directly to research. The exceptions permit state and local educational authorities to nonconsensually disclose personally identifiable information from education records to organizations conducting studies "for or on behalf of" schools, school districts, or postsecondary institutions. Studies must be for the purpose of developing, validating, or administering predictive tests; administering student aid programs; or improving instruction (34 CFR § 99.31(a)(6).

Release of data for research purposes must also include a written agreement that identifies and codifies the terms of data sharing—for instance, regarding specific data elements to be released, use of the data, and compliance with requirements for destroying data . Notably, the most recent amendments to FERPA (January 2012) were made with the explicit purpose of "allowing the effective use of student data" and specifically point to statewide longitudinal data systems as the vehicle for achieving it.[5]

Health Insurance Portability and Accountability Act (HIPAA) of 1996, Privacy Rule[6] The federal Health Insurance Portability and Accountability Act Privacy Rule (45 CFR § 160 and § 164) governs health data and stipulates that any researcher, referred to as a "business associate," is required to have a data use agreement that includes certain protections for information, such as internal practices, books, and records, including policies and procedures and protected health information.

In general, a business associate is a person or organization other than a member of a covered entity's workforce that performs certain functions or activities on behalf of, or provides certain services to, a covered entity that involves the use or disclosure of individually identifiable health information. The business associate functions or activities on behalf of a covered entity include claims processing, data analysis, utilization review, and billing.

The Privacy Rule requires that the covered entity include certain protections for the information in a business associate agreement—a DUA, in the case of the YDA or other integrated longitudinal data systems. (In certain circumstances governmental entities may use alternative means to achieve the same protections.) In the business associate contract (or DUA), a covered entity must impose specified written safeguards on the individually identifiable health information used or disclosed by its business associates.

California State Regulations

The following regulations provide a governing structure for individually identifiable data in the state of California, but each state has addressed this issue differently. Therefore, comparable regulations should be consulted depending on the location of the data-sharing relationship. Additionally, many of the state laws mirror in some ways their counterpart federal laws.

California Civil Code Section 1798.24–1798.24b The California Civil Code stipulates that no state agency may share personal client information unless there is adequate written assurance that information will be used solely for statistical research or reporting purposes. In addition, the institution receiving personal information from the agency must have its data security protocol approved by the state Committee for the Protection of Human Subjects (CPHS) or a CPHS-empowered institutional review board.

Specifically, agencies may not release personal information in such a way that the released information would enable the identification of any individual unless the information is released in the following manner:

- (h) "To a person who has provided the agency with advance, adequate written assurance that the information will be used solely for statistical research or reporting purposes, but only if the information to be disclosed is in a form that will not identify any individual." (In the case of the YDA, the DUA would act as "written assurance," and as with the federal Privacy Act, data would need to be encrypted during transfer.)
- (t) (1) "To the University of California, a nonprofit educational institution, or, in the case of education-related data, another nonprofit entity conducting scientific research, provided the request for information is approved by the CPHS for the California Health and Human Services Agency (CHHSA) or an institutional review board that has a written agreement with CPHS. The approval required under this subdivision shall include a review and determination that all the following criteria have been satisfied:
  - The researcher has provided a plan sufficient to protect personal information from improper use and disclosures, including sufficient administrative, physical, and technical safeguards to

protect personal information from reasonable anticipated threats to the security or confidentiality of the information.

– The researcher has provided a sufficient plan to destroy or return all personal information as soon as it is no longer needed for the research project, unless the researcher has demonstrated an ongoing need for the personal information for the research project and has provided a long-term plan sufficient to protect the confidentiality of that information." (The above two stipulations are similar to HIPAA in requiring a plan or internal practices for data security.)

– "The researcher has provided sufficient written assurances that the personal information will not be reused or disclosed to any other person or entity, or used in any manner, not approved in the research protocol, except as required by law or for authorized oversight of the research project."

California State Education Code, 49073-49079, 49079.6.b The California State Education Code includes provisions for the release of student-level data both by school districts and by the state Department of Education. Specifically, school districts have discretion over student data[8] in the following ways:

• In determining what information can be released to researchers
• In determining who or which organizations can receive information
• In denying requests based on pupils' *best interests*
• In releasing information for current and former students
• In providing statistical data from which no pupil may be identified to research organizations when it would be in the best educational interests of pupils
• In releasing information from pupil records to organizations conducting studies for, or on behalf of, educational agencies or institutions for the purpose of developing, validating, or administering predictive tests, administering student aid programs, and

improving instruction, provided that the studies are conducted in a manner that will not permit the personal identification of pupils or their parents by persons other than representatives of the organizations, and that the information will be destroyed when no longer needed for the purpose for which it is obtained. (This point mirrors FERPA, allowing for YDA analyses under specific circumstances and conditions.)

The code also requires districts to give notice at least once a year about the categories of information that a school plans to release as well as about who the recipients will be, and it stipulates that they cannot release information if a parent has requested the school district not to do so.

At the state level, the California Department of Education can release individually identifiable data to "qualified researchers from nonprofit entities" on behalf of local educational agencies under the following circumstances:[9]

- If the department establishes an education data team to work with researchers conducting studies to improve instruction
- If agreements between researchers and the department include guidelines for data control, destruction of data after use, and protection against any misuse of data, including third-party transfer

Child Welfare and Institutions Code, 10850, Confidentiality of Records[10]　In general, the Child Welfare and Institutions Code covers the welfare of individuals receiving any form of public social service (including child welfare, such as foster care). The following mandates cover use of individually identified data for the YDA or other research purposes:

- Research organizations requesting information must provide a written guarantee that they will comply with the conditions and protections of Welfare and Institutions Code section 10850 and the California Department of Social Services Manual of Policies and Procedures,[11] Division 19 (Confidentiality of Information).
- The State Department of Social Services is entitled to make rules and regulations governing the storage and use of all documents

related to administering public social service laws. The rules and regulations extend to all state departments and may specify releasing or exchanging information with public or private agencies for the purposes of provision of social services; and for making case records available for research purposes, as long as release of the records does not reveal the identity of applicants for or recipients of public social services and will not release any personal information that would allow for linking it to the individual to whom it pertains, unless the department has complied with subdivision (t) of Section 1798.24 of the Civil Code (see above).

APPENDIX 2

SAMPLE DATA USE AGREEMENT
FOR SCHOOL DISTRICTS

Agreement for Confidential Data Exchange
Between Generic School District and the John
W. Gardner Center for Youth and Their
Communities at Stanford University

This Data Exchange and Confidentiality Agreement ("Agreement") between Generic School District (hereinafter referred to as GENERIC SD), The Board of Trustees of the Leland Stanford Junior University by and through its John W. Gardner Center for Youth and Their Communities (hereinafter referred to as JGC) describes the means to be used by JGC to ensure the confidentiality and security of information and data exchanged between GENERIC SD and JGC for the purposes stated below.

I. GENERAL TERMS

A. Purpose

The JGC has developed the Youth Data Archive (YDA), an archive of matched longitudinal administrative data for conducting policy analyses for County leaders and practitioners. Policy questions to be addressed using the YDA will be developed in collaboration with participating public agencies and representatives of local community-based organizations. To ensure that the YDA is a valuable resource for all agencies contributing data, the project may also work with GENERIC SD to identify one or more additional research questions that will be included in the project scope on behalf of GENERIC SD.

B. Nature of Data

To further the achievement of the above stated purpose, GENERIC SD will at its discretion provide JGC with data extracts from the GENERIC SD data systems to include data elements identified in Attachment A, as well as any additional items required to answer research questions defined by GENERIC SD alone or with other participants in the YDA.

These data extracts will include historical information wherever possible. Additional data elements may be provided at the discretion of GENERIC SD.

Because the YDA will match individual student level data, these data are expected to contain confidential information, the disclosure of which is restricted by a provision of law. Some examples of "confidential information" include, but are not limited to, "personal information" about individuals as defined in California Civil Code Section 1798.3 of the Information Practices Act and "personal information" about students as defined by the Code of Federal Regulations CFR Title 34 Volume 1 Part 99.3.

C. Transfer of Data

GENERIC SD and JGC shall use a secure, mutually agreed upon means and schedule for transferring confidential information. GENERIC SD will create data extracts and validate the data. Extracts will be updated using a mutually agreed upon schedule. At no time will data be sent electronically to or from the parties.

D. Period of Agreement

This Agreement shall be effective per specifications in Attachment B, unless terminated earlier by either party pursuant to Section F.

E. JGC Responsibilities

JGC agrees to the following confidentiality statements:

1. JGC acknowledges that these data are confidential data and proprietary to GENERIC SD, and agree to protect such information from unauthorized disclosures and comply with all applicable confidentiality laws including but not limited to, the Health Insurance Portability and Accountability Act (HIPAA), the California Education Code and the Family Education Rights and Privacy Act (FERPA) as set forth in this agreement. JGC is responsible for complying with all District, Local, State and Federal confidentiality applicable laws and regulations.

2. JGC will use appropriate safeguards to prevent the use or disclosure of the information other than as provided by this data use Agreement.

3. JGC shall (a) instruct all staff with access to confidential information about the requirements for handling confidential information (b) provide all staff with access to confidential information statements of organizational policies and procedures for the protection of human subjects and data confidentiality and (c) notify staff of the sanctions against unauthorized disclosure or use of confidential and private information. JGC will ensure that all staff and subcontractors to whom they provide the limited data sets obtained under this Agreement, agrees to the same restrictions and conditions that apply to JGC in this Agreement with respect to such information. Other than as provided herein, no confidential data will be released by JGC.

4. JGC shall not assign this Agreement or any portion thereof to a third party without the prior written consent of GENERIC SD, and any attempted assignment without such prior written consent in violation of this Section shall automatically terminate this Agreement.

5. JGC will use any information which could potentially allow the identification of any individual only for the purpose of creating

the data sets using aggregate data and analyzing the data. JGC will not use or further disclose the information accessed or received other than as permitted by this Data Use Agreement or as otherwise required by law. Information which could potentially identify any individuals will be maintained in a separate data set and used only to create and update the linked data archive.

6. JGC will report only aggregate data and will not report any individual data, nor will data be reported in a manner that permits indirect identification of any individual. This paragraph will survive the termination of this Agreement.

7. JGC will not contact the individuals included in the data sets.

8. JGC agrees to obtain written approval from GENERIC SD prior to engaging any subcontractors to perform any services requiring access to any individually identifiable information.

9. JGC shall not re-disclose any individual-level data with or without identifying information to any other requesting individuals, agencies, or organizations without prior written authorization by GENERIC SD

10. JGC shall use the data only for the purpose stated above. These data shall not be used for personal gain or profit.

11. JGC shall keep all information furnished by GENERIC SD in a space physically and electronically secure from unauthorized access. Information and data shall be stored and processed in a way that unauthorized persons cannot retrieve nor alter the information by means of a computer, remote terminal, or other means. No data will be stored on laptop computers or other portable computing devices or media, e.g., flash drives, etc.

12. JGC shall permit examination and on-site inspections by GENERIC SD upon reasonable advance notice for the purpose of ascertaining whether the terms of this Agreement are being met.

F. Termination

1. This Agreement may be terminated as follows, after notification via the United States Postal Service (certified mail or registered

mail) or recognized overnight delivery service (e.g., UPS, DHL or FedEx):

   a. By JGC or GENERIC SD immediately in the event of a material breach of this Agreement by the other party.

   b. By JGC or GENERIC SD upon 30 days notice to the other party.

2. At the termination of this Agreement or upon written request of GENERIC SD, whichever is earlier, JGC shall return all confidential and/or sensitive information promptly and destroy all copies or derivations of the confidential and/or sensitive information utilizing an approved method of confidential destruction, including shredding, burning or certified/witnessed destruction for physical materials and verified erasure of magnetic media using approved methods of electronic file destruction.

G. General Understanding

1. This Agreement contains the entire understanding of the parties and may only be amended in writing signed by the parties.

2. This Agreement shall be governed by and construed under the laws of the State of California.

3. Any waiver by any party of the violation of any provision of this Agreement shall not bar any action for subsequent violations of the Agreement.

Signed:

For generic school district

For the John W. Gardner Center for Youth and Their Communities

_____

Name, title

_____

Amy Gerstein, Executive Director

_____

Date

_____

Date

II. ORGANIZATION-SPECIFIC AGREEMENTS: ATTACHMENTS

Attachment A: Specific Data Elements

- Student identifiers
    - Student name
    - Student date of birth
    - Student identifier
    - Address
- School enrollment
    - Application Terms
    - Enrollment Terms
    - Registration Attempts
- Demographics and Academic Markers
    - Educational Level (HS, AA, Bachelor's)
    - Educational Goal
    - Educational Status (new, continuing)
    - Ethnicity
    - Gender
    - ESL Student Status (ESL or native speaker)
    - Basic Skills Status and Entering Level in ESL, English and mathematics
    - Full/Part Time
    - Work Hours
    - Reported High School of Origin
    - Division of Origin (Credit or Noncredit)
- Academic achievement
    - Units attempted and completed
    - Grades by subject area, online versus traditional, basic skills versus degree applicable, transferable to UC, CSU
    - Cumulative GPA, GPA by semester (if available)
    - Location of Classes
    - Placement and Assessment data
    - Term and Year Persistence
    - Course Repetitions

Advancement through the gateway Sequences

Graduation with either a AA/AS Degree or Certificate

Transfer to Other Colleges

- Student services participation

    Intervention Program participation—include hours or days
        attended

    Matriculation Services Received

- Disciplinary data

    Probationary Status

Attachment B: Period of Agreement

This agreement shall be effective beginning XX April 2012 through XX April 2014, unless terminated earlier by either party pursuant to Section F. The effective dates of this agreement may be modified by written amendment subject to acceptance of both parties.

Attachment C: Various Other Organization-Specific Agreements

Re E. JGC Responsibilities

JGC will not conduct any analyses using GENERIC SD data without prior approval by an authorized GENERIC SD representative. JGC will not publish findings obtained using GENERIC SD data without prior approval by an authorized GENERIC SD representative. GENERIC SD shall designate the following person(s) as authorized representatives for the YDA:

Name _____ Title _____

Name _____ Title _____

Name _____ Title _____

APPENDIX 3

SAMPLE DATA USE AGREEMENT FOR ORGANIZATIONS OTHER THAN SCHOOL DISTRICTS

Agreement for Confidential Data Exchange Between Generic Organization and the John W. Gardner Center for Youth and Their Communities at Stanford University

This Data Exchange and Confidentiality Agreement ("Agreement") between GENERIC ORGANIZATION (hereinafter referred to as ORGANIZA-TION), The Board of Trustees of the Leland Stanford Junior University by and through its John W. Gardner Center for Youth and Their Communities (hereinafter referred to as JGC) describes the means to be used by JGC to ensure the confidentiality and security of information and data exchanged between ORGANIZATION and JGC for the purposes stated below.

I. GENERAL TERMS

A. Purpose

The JGC has developed the Youth Data Archive (YDA), an archive of matched longitudinal administrative data for conducting policy analyses for County leaders and practitioners. Policy questions to be addressed using the YDA will be developed in collaboration with participating public agencies and representatives of local community-based organizations. To ensure that the YDA is a valuable resource for all agencies contributing data, the project may also work with ORGANIZATION to identify one or more additional research questions that will be included in the project scope on behalf of ORGANIZATION.

B. Nature of Data

To further the achievement of the above stated purpose, ORGANIZATION will at its discretion provide JGC with data extracts from the ORGANIZATION data systems to include data elements identified in Attachment A, as well as any additional items required to answer research questions defined by ORGANIZATION alone or with other participants in the YDA.

These data extracts will include historical information wherever possible. Additional data elements may be provided at the discretion of ORGANIZATION.

Because the YDA will match individual student level data, these data are expected to contain confidential information, the disclosure of which is restricted by a provision of law. Some examples of "confidential information" include, but are not limited to, "personal information" about individuals as defined in California Civil Code Section 1798.3 of the Information Practices Act and "personal information" about students as defined by the Code of Federal Regulations CFR Title 34 Volume 1 Part 99.3.

C. Transfer of Data

ORGANIZATION and JGC shall use a secure, mutually agreed upon means and schedule for transferring confidential information. ORGANIZATION will create data extracts and validate the data. Extracts will be updated using a mutually agreed upon schedule. At no time will data be sent electronically to or from the parties.

D. Period of Agreement

This Agreement shall be effective per specifications in Attachment B, unless terminated earlier by either party pursuant to Section F.

E. JGC Responsibilities

JGC agrees to the following confidentiality statements:

1. JGC acknowledges that these data are confidential data and proprietary to ORGANIZATION, and agree to protect such information from unauthorized disclosures and comply with all applicable confidentiality laws including but not limited to, the Health Insurance Portability and Accountability Act (HIPAA), the California Education Code and the Family Education Rights and Privacy Act (FERPA) as set forth in this agreement. JGC is responsible for complying with all District, Local, State and Federal confidentiality applicable laws and regulations.

2. JGC will use appropriate safeguards to prevent the use or disclosure of the information other than as provided by this data use Agreement.

3. JGC shall (a) instruct all staff with access to confidential information about the requirements for handling confidential information (b) provide all staff with access to confidential information statements of organizational policies and procedures for the protection of human subjects and data confidentiality and (c) notify staff of the sanctions against unauthorized disclosure or use of confidential and private information. JGC will ensure that all staff and subcontractors to whom they provide the limited data sets obtained under this Agreement, agrees to the same restrictions and conditions that apply to JGC in this Agreement with respect to such information. Other than as provided herein, no confidential data will be released by JGC.

4. JGC shall not assign this Agreement or any portion thereof to a third party without the prior written consent of ORGANIZATION,

and any attempted assignment without such prior written consent in violation of this Section shall automatically terminate this Agreement.

5. JGC will use any information which could potentially allow the identification of any individual only for the purpose of creating the data sets using aggregate data and analyzing the data. JGC will not use or further disclose the information accessed or received other than as permitted by this Data Use Agreement or as otherwise required by law. Information which could potentially identify any individuals will be maintained in a separate data set and used only to create and update the linked data archive.

6. JGC will report only aggregate data and will not report any individual data, nor will data be reported in a manner that permits indirect identification of any individual. This paragraph will survive the termination of this Agreement.

7. JGC will not contact the individuals included in the data sets.

8. JGC agrees to obtain written approval from ORGANIZATION prior to engaging any subcontractors to perform any services requiring access to any individually identifiable information.

9. JGC shall not re-disclose any individual-level data with or without identifying information to any other requesting individuals, agencies, or organizations without prior written authorization by ORGANIZATION

10. JGC shall use the data only for the purpose stated above. These data shall not be used for personal gain or profit.

11. JGC shall keep all information furnished by ORGANIZATION in a space physically and electronically secure from unauthorized access. Information and data shall be stored and processed in a way that unauthorized persons cannot retrieve nor alter the information by means of a computer, remote terminal, or other means. No data will be stored on laptop computers or other portable computing devices or media, e.g., flash drives, etc.

12. JGC shall permit examination and on-site inspections by ORGA-NIZATION upon reasonable advance notice for the purpose of ascertaining whether the terms of this Agreement are being met.

F. Termination

1. This Agreement may be terminated as follows, after notification via the United States Postal Service (certified mail or registered mail) or recognized overnight delivery service (e.g., UPS, DHL or FedEx):
   a. By JGC or ORGANIZATION immediately in the event of a material breach of this Agreement by the other party.
   b. By JGC or ORGANIZATION upon 30 days notice to the other party.
2. At the termination of this Agreement or upon written request of ORGANIZATION, whichever is earlier, JGC shall return all confidential and/or sensitive information promptly and destroy all copies or derivations of the confidential and/or sensitive information utilizing an approved method of confidential destruction, including shredding, burning or certified/witnessed destruction for physical materials and verified erasure of magnetic media using approved methods of electronic file destruction.

G. General Understanding

1. This Agreement contains the entire understanding of the parties and may only be amended in writing signed by the parties.
2. This Agreement shall be governed by and construed under the laws of the State of California.
3. Any waiver by any party of the violation of any provision of this Agreement shall not bar any action for subsequent violations of the Agreement.

Signed:

For Organization   *For the John W. Gardner Center for*
                                      Youth and Their Communities

_____   _____

Name, Title   Amy Gerstein, Executive Director

_____   _____

Date   Date

II. ORGANIZATION-SPECIFIC AGREEMENTS: ATTACHMENTS

Attachment A: Specific Data Elements

- Student identifiers and demographic information
    Student name
    Student date of birth
    CBO identifier
    Address
    Ethnicity
    Gender
    Parent/Guardian name (if available) or additional family
        information
    Current and past schools attended
- Membership
    Enrollment date
    Withdrawal date pending inclusion of variable in data
        collection
    Specific dates attended
    Type of programs or services utilized
    Reason for withdrawal

Attachment B: Period of Agreement

This agreement shall be effective beginning XX Month 2012 through XX Month 2014, unless terminated earlier by either party pursuant to Section F. The effective dates of this agreement may be modified by written amendment subject to acceptance of both parties.

Attachment C: Various Other Organization-Specific Agreements

Re E: JGC Responsibilities

JGC will not conduct any analyses using ORGANIZATION data without prior approval by an authorized ORGANIZATION representative. JGC will not publish findings obtained using ORGANIZATION data without prior approval by an authorized ORGANIZATION representative. ORGANIZATION shall designate the following person(s) as authorized representatives for the YDA:

Name _____ Title _____

Name _____ Title _____

Name _____ Title _____

SECURE SERVER DOCUMENTATION AND INFORMATION SECURITY POLICIES

John W. Gardner Center for Youth
and Their Communities Server Documentation
and Information Security Policies

1. DATA CLASSIFICATION, ACCESS, TRANSMITTAL AND STORAGE

Stanford takes seriously its commitment to respect and protect the privacy of its students, alumni, faculty and staff, as well as to protect the confidentiality of information important to the University's academic and research mission. For that reason, Stanford has identified three categories of non-public information for the purpose of determining who is allowed to access the information and what security precautions must be taken to protect the information against unauthorized access. The categories are listed in table A4.1.

Table A4.1 Stanford University categorization of non-public information

	Prohibited information	Restricted information	Confidential information
Information classification guideline	Information is classified as "Prohibited" if protection of the information is required by law/regulation or Stanford is required to self-report to the government and/or provide notice to the individual if information is inappropriately accessed. If a file which would otherwise be considered to be Restricted or Confidential contains any element of Prohibited Information, the entire file is considered to be Prohibited Information.	Information is classified as "Restricted" if (i) it would otherwise qualify as "Prohibited" but it has been determined by the DGB that prohibiting information storage on Computing Equipment *would significantly reduce* faculty/staff/student effectiveness when acting in support of Stanford's mission and/or (ii) it is listed as Restricted in the "Classification of Common Data Elements," below.	Information is classified as "Confidential" if (i) it is not considered to be Prohibited or Restricted and is not generally available to the public, or (ii) it is listed as Confidential in the "Classification of Common Data Elements," below.
Classification of common data elements	• Social Security Numbers • Credit card numbers • Financial account numbers, such as checking or investment account numbers • Driver's license numbers • Health insurance policy ID numbers	• Health information, including Protected Health Information (PHI) • Passport and visa numbers • Export controlled information under U.S. laws	• Student records • Research data • Faculty/staff employment applications, personnel files, benefits information, salary, birth date, and personal contact information • Admission applications • Donor contact information and non-public gift amounts • Privileged attorney-client communications • Non-public Stanford policies and policy manuals • Stanford internal memos and email, and non-public reports, budgets, plans, and financial information • Non-public contracts • University and employee ID numbers

	Prohibited information	Restricted information	Confidential information
	Access only with permission from the DGB or the VP for Business Affairs.	Access limited to those permitted under law, regulation and Stanford's policies, and with a need to know.	Access limited to those with a need to know.
Transmission	NIST-approved encryption is required when transmitting information through a network. Third party email services are not appropriate for transmitting Prohibited information. Prohibited numbers may be Masked instead of encrypted.	NIST-approved encryption is required when transmitting information through a network. Third party email services are not appropriate for transmitting Restricted information. Restricted numbers may be Masked instead of encrypted.	NIST-approved encryption is strongly recommended when transmitting information through a network. Third party email services are discouraged for transmitting Confidential information.
Storage	Prohibited on Computing Equipment unless approved by the DGB. If DGB approves, NIST-approved encryption is required on Computing Equipment. Prohibited numbers may be Masked instead of encrypted. NIST-approved encryption is also required if the information is not stored on a Qualified Machine. Third party processing or storage services are not appropriate for receiving or storing Prohibited information unless approved by the DGB.	NIST-approved encryption is required if information is stored on Computing Equipment. Restricted numbers may be Masked instead of encrypted. NIST-approved encryption is also required if the information is not stored on a Qualified Machine. Third party processing or storage services are not appropriate for receiving or storing Restricted information unless approved by the DGB.	Encryption of Confidential information is strongly recommended. Level of required protection of Confidential information is either pursuant to Stanford policy or at the discretion of the owner or custodian of the information. If appropriate level of protection is not known, check before storing Confidential information unencrypted. Third party processing or storage services may receive or store Confidential data if Stanford has a valid contract with the vendor that includes the standard clauses specified in the ASP Security Requirements.

All information which does not fall into one of these categories is considered to be "public". Public information includes, but is not limited to, SUNet ID, information available on or through Stanford's website if accessible without SUNet ID, certain policy and procedure manuals designated by the owner as "public," campus maps, job postings, certain University contact information not designated by the individual as "private" in StanfordYou, etc. No encryption or other protection is required for public information; however, care should always be taken to use all University information appropriately.

2. STANFORD NETWORK

2.1 Overview

The Stanford University Network (SUNet) consists of local networks within buildings and a backbone network that connects the local networks to each other and to networks off campus. The backbone is designed and operated by Networking Systems, a division of Shared Communication Services, part of Information Technology Services. Network services within individual buildings are the responsibility of the departments that occupy those buildings, unless support is purchased from IT Services.

For academic and administrative buildings, we provide and support the data communication infrastructure to the facility entrance. Through the Net2switch program, we provide data communication infrastructure within the academic and administrative buildings. For student residences, Networking Systems supports the data communication infrastructure to the service outlets in student rooms. Networking Systems maintains off-campus connectivity through multiple internet connections as well as Internet2.

The SUNet backbone consists of two backbone switch/routers and ten operational zones. Each operational zone consists of a redundant pair of operational zone routers, a redundant pair of operational zone firewalls, and a redundant pair of operational zone distribution switches. Each operational zone services 30 to 50 departmental networks. In order to further enhance availability, the redundant network equipment is geographically dispersed in multiple electronic communications hubs around campus.

All connections between the operational zone equipment, as well as from each operational zone to the backbone routers, operate at 10Gbps. Departmental networks connect into the operational zone at 1Gbps.

For off-campus connections in the Palo Alto area, it is possible to make high-speed fiber-optic connections by contracting for the use of the fiber plant run by the City of Palo Alto Utilities. Where fiber is not available, connections back to campus can be made using serial lines provided by the phone company (e.g., ATT/SBC/Pac*Bell). Typically these lines run at DS1 (T1) speeds, around 1.5 megabits per second. For home connections, IT Services has a Stanford-managed DSL offering, which provides the home users a direct connection to SUNet.

The SUNet backbone connects to CENIC, Internet2 HPR, DC, NLR, and the commercial Internet. The SUNet backbone has a 10-Gigabit connection to the NRENs (National Research and Education Networks) via the HPR (High-Performance Research) network run by CENIC (Corporation for Educational Networks in California). Stanford has multiple 1-Gigabit connections to CENIC, which provides access to both Internet2 and NLR (National Lambda Rail) networks, both of which run at 10-Gigabit for educational institutions in California. Stanford also has a commercial Internet connection provided by Cogent ISP for traffic destined to locations not reachable via the CENIC peering connections.

2.2 Virtual Private Network

Virtual Private Network (VPN) is a remote access technology that creates a private encrypted connection over the Internet between a single host and Stanford's private network, SUNet. Stanford's VPN service allows Stanford affiliates to connect to the campus from any available network connection almost anywhere including from home, from many hotels, and even from within some company networks.

The VPN service provides users with a Stanford IP address, thereby making access to restricted services possible. Examples include:

- Users on the MedSchool and Hospital networks who need to access resources on the University network (SUNET).

- Users connecting from corporate networks.

If connection is established over wireless network or comes from outside the Stanford network (for example, at a conference), it is recommended to use Stanford VPN to connect to the Stanford network. If you are using a wired computer and are on the Stanford network, it is generally sufficient to use encrypted protocols such as SSH, HTTPS, and IMAPS instead of VPN. (Using VPN in this case would not measurably improve security.)

2.3 Network Access Control

The Stanford University Network Access Control (SUNAC) service offers a standardized approach for addressing the security needs of faculty, staff, and students who require remote connectivity.

Highly granular and configurable, the service allows LNAs (Local Network Administrators) to control remote access to departmental resources located behind IT Services-managed firewalls. Using Workgroup Manager, access can be granted to any faculty, staff member, or student with a SUNet ID and password.

The SUNAC architecture and operational processes have been reviewed and approved by the Information Security Office. Security policy is put forth by the University. The systems administration team will adhere to all security policies documented in the Stanford Administrative Guide.

3. ITS STORAGE

This service provides standard ways for individuals and groups to share files across intranets and the Internet. The Individual & Group File Storage service uses the CIFS (Common Internet File System) protocol to provide access to central file services.

By using a remote file-access protocol that is compatible with the way applications already share data on local disks and network file servers, Individual & Group File Storage enables collaboration on the Internet. It can be a good way to have secure and sharable file storage for groups and departments.

May be used to store public and Confidential Data, as defined by the Stanford University Information Security Office.

4. ITS DATA CENTER

IT Services provides hosting services for campus clients who want to operate their equipment in a secure, centrally-managed data center. This controlled environment is run as a university resource, providing secure and reliable services for university communications, computing, and data applications.

Technical Facilities supports a data center in Forsythe Hall that provides these hosting services. The Forsythe Hall data center is characterized by:

- Secured entry
- 24/7 monitoring
- Access to SUNet services
- Access to SAN and NAS services
- Controlled humidity and temperature
- Monitored environmental control systems
- Fire detection and fire suppression
- Water intrusion sensors
- Sufficient power for all installed equipment
- An Uninterruptible Power Supply (UPS) to protect against power anomalies
- Battery backup and standby generators to maintain normal operations during a utility outage
- Preexisting, standard 19-inch racks with full cable management

5. WINDOWS INFRASTRUCTURE

5.1 Stanford Domain

The Stanford Windows Infrastructure is built on Microsoft's Active Directory Domain Services and the Windows Server 2008 R2 operating system.

Domain controllers hold account and group information. There are at least two domain controllers for each domain in the Stanford Windows Infrastructure. In addition, four infrastructure domain controllers serve as "global catalog servers", which hold the subset of searchable information of all directory objects. A global catalog server is involved in almost every login.

The network designed for the domain controllers is pictured below. Each pair of on-campus domain controllers is co-located—one in Near East ECH, one in West ECH—with a dedicated Gigabit fiber connection for directory replication and other domain traffic. The on-campus domain controllers are on an isolated subnet. There is a DNS cache local to each server room, so network or even DNS outages have minimal effect. This network is connected directly to the Stanford network backbone, so multiple paths are always available.

5.2 Authentication

Stanford University offers a multitude of computing services to the Stanford community. To access many of these services people must enter their SUNet ID username and password. The SUNet ID establishes their affiliation with Stanford and their right to use its computing services. Each SUNet ID is represented as a principal in both the Stanford Windows Infrastructure and the heimdal-based Kerberos5 realm (stanford.edu)

5.3 Directory

The SUNet Registry and Stanford Directory together form the University's primary repository of directory information for people, organizations, groups, applications, and accounts. The Active Directory of the Windows Infrastructure is a subscriber to the SUNet Registry/Directory.

The information in the Active Directory is replicated one way from the Stanford Registry. Modification of this data must be done at the authoritative source. As mandated by the federal law known as FERPA, Stanford is liable for the privacy of personal data. This means that universities must honor student's requests to protect their personal information. The Stanford Registry therefore has privacy settings that are mimicked in Active

Directory for applicable personal data. Security ACLs are set on personal data attributes to protect both the privacy and the integrity of this data. For this reason, some data in Active Directory can only be seen by some groups. Additionally, replicated personal information attributes on user accounts are non-writable in Active Directory; this ensures that the Stanford Registry remains the single provider of personal data at the University.

6. WORKSTATION SECURITY

6.1 Information Security Office (ISO)

The Information Security Office and IT Services provide central network and computing security services that include blocking traffic at the campus network perimeter and at firewalls, preventive scanning, automated and streamlined systems for incident response, and timely notifications and alerts.

The Information Security Office oversees the Stanford community's efforts to protect its computing and information assets and to comply with information-related laws, regulations, and policies. The office reports to the university's senior management through the Office of the Vice President for Business Affairs and Chief Financial Officer.

The ISO's approach to security is more proactive than reactive, although we naturally give priority response to incidents that have institution-level impact or that require university-wide coordination.

ISO's current focus is securing systems that affect a majority of the university, including central administrative systems and the campus data network. The ISO gives special priority to systems containing data classified as Prohibited or Restricted (see the Data Classification).

6.2 Security Patch Management

Stanford uses IBM Tivoli Endpoint Manger—built on BigFix technology—to deploy patches and updates to Windows and Macintosh computers. BigFix also provides a consistent and reliable way to remotely configure power settings. BigFix is administered by IT Services in collaboration with others across the University.

The BigFix Patch Management service provides the following benefits:

- It allows Stanford to install critical security patches on computers as soon as they're made available by Microsoft and Apple and tested here.
- Release of patches occurs after broad campus-wide testing and follows a rigorous, but rapid, procedure.
- BigFix is an agent-based software solution. Each computer communicates with the BigFix server to determine its patch status. The server automatically applies appropriate updates once they have been released.
- Certain basic inventory information about the computer—such as the presence or absence of critical security updates, IP address, operating system, and some hardware data—is collected. A complete list of collected information is always available.

6.3 Virus Protection

Sophos Anti-Virus is Stanford's site-licensed anti-malware software. It can protect your computer against viruses, adware/spyware, and other malicious software.

6.4 Managed Desktops

Managed Desktop is a service offering from IT Services for use by technical support staff. It enables departments to centrally manage their desktop computers using automated processes.

Some of the functions performed by Managed Desktop include:

- Real-time maintenance of security settings
- Configuration management
- Software version control
- Automated patching and updating

Managed Desktop service may be used with Prohibited, Restricted, and Confidential Data, as defined by the Stanford University Information Security Office.

6.5 Encryption

The purpose of the Stanford Whole Disk Encryption (SWDE) service is to protect Restricted and Confidential Data that must be stored on faculty and staff computers.

The Stanford Whole Disk Encryption service is for both Windows and Macintosh desktop and laptop computers. This service secures data using standard NIST-approved encryption of the computer hard disk. Once installed, all files are automatically encrypted. The data is protected while the computer is in standby or hibernation mode as long as the hard disk is password protected. This solution additionally supports encryption of USB drives.

While there is no single solution to protect the university's data, Stanford Whole Disk Encryption protects all data on a hard disk from unauthorized access in the event the computer is lost or stolen.

- Only the SWDE passphrase holder is authorized to access the data, which protects the data if your computer is lost or stolen.
- Every computer using SWDE automatically checks in with a logging and administrative server on a regular basis. In the event of loss or theft of a computer with Restricted Data, Stanford policy requires notification of the Information Security Office (ISO). ISO in turn will use the log to determine if a lost or stolen computer is a "reportable" event, possibly requiring notification of persons whose data may have been lost or stolen.
- In the event you lose or forget your passphrase, the IT Services Help Desk will assist you in accessing your computer so that you can reset your passphrase.
- If necessary, the whole disk can be unencrypted (with the assistance of IT Services to guarantee the integrity of the audit trail).

7. JGC SERVER

The security arrangements on JGC server were reviewed and approved by Information Security Office, which also contributed to the initial planning of the service.

JGC server is running Microsoft Windows 2008R2 Server operating system and utilizes Terminal Services to allow remote access to the JGC users.

Server Security Setup

- The server is located in ITS Data Center, which provides required security arrangements like controlled access, security camera monitoring, locked server racks.
- Four levels of firewalls control server access: Stanford perimeter firewall, administrative firewall, network access control and local server firewall.
- Administrative firewall is configured to deny access to any ports except RDP (Remote Desktop Protocol), which is used by JGC users. All outbound connections from the server except RDP connections are also denied.
- Use of RDP as single protocol for data access and transfer narrows the possible attack vector to minimum possible.
- JGC server requires RDP clients to establish SSL encrypted channel to connect to the server. This ensures safety of data in transit from user's workstations to the server.
- To access the server users must connect through Virtual Private Network (VPN). VPN connection requires installation of the client and authentication with SUNet ID and password.
- Stanford University Network Access control requires authentication from remote users before they are allowed to access the network, where the server is located. Users are authenticated with their SUNet ID and password.
- Authentication to VPN and SUNAC services leverages secure Stanford Directory Infrastructure to verify the identity of the users.
- To login to the server separate user id and password are required. Authentication relies on accounts stored in Stanford Windows domain. Dual authentication with different user names and passwords ensures that even if one set of credentials is compromised, data security is not impacted.

- Unprivileged user accounts are locked down and provide access only to applications and areas of the server, which are necessary for research data storage and processing.
- Server is regularly backed up using CrashPlan software. Backup data is encrypted at the time of collection and before it leaves the server.

7.1 Audit

- The server has Application, System and Security logging enabled.
- Following security information is logged:
  Account logon events
  Account management events
  Directory service access
  System events
- Logs are backed up and stored for a year.

7.2 Data Backup

JGC server uses CrashPlan backup software to continuously backup data and user files. Retention policy is as follows:
- Backup frequency: every 4hr
- Versions to keep from last week: every 4hr
- Version to keep from last three months: every day
- Versions to keep from last year: every week

7.3 Contingency Planning

Data on the server is continuously backed up to ITS Storage, which provides both on-site and off-site locations. Mirroring of the on-site location to off-site is happening nightly. Data can be easily restored in case of server hardware or software failure.

Snapshots of the system volume are created nightly and stored on ITS Storage. Image of the system volume can be quickly restored to the new server in case of hardware or system failure.

7.4 Workstations Accessing the Server

Workstations, which are used to access the server are:

- Bound to Stanford Active Directory domain.
- Run antivirus software.
- Run patch management software.
- Have their hard disks encrypted.
- Upload and removal of the data on the server are allowed from a single workstation used from secure location.

Analysts and administration of John W. Gardner Center implement these policies.

7.5 Data Deletion

After uploading data to the JGC server, the media which was used to transport the data, must be handled in one of the following ways:

- Physically destroyed.
- Encrypted. Stanford full disk encryption service provides the facility to encrypt the data on external magnetic media.
- Wiped according to the DoD standards.

Receiving of the data, upload and further handling of the media is performed by analysts of John W. Gardner Center.

Data received from different agencies is stored on the server and backed up separately. On request from the agency to delete data, it is deleted from:

- Server storage by server administrator.
- Backups by server administrator.

NOTES

Chapter 1

1. Foundations' generous and early support was essential since at its beginning the YDA represented little more than an idea that was well supported by literature and experience, but one with little concrete demonstration of practicality or value. These initial investments came from the Atlantic Philanthropies, the William and Flora Hewlett Foundation, the James Irvine Foundation, the Ewing Marion Kauffman Foundation, the David and Lucile Packard Foundation, the Skoll Foundation, and the Walton Family Foundation.

2. See http://www.gse.upenn.edu/child/projects/kids.

3. See http://dfcyr.hartford.gov/index.php/youthservices/hartfordconnects.

4. See http://ccsr.uchicago.edu/ content/index.php.

5. See http://edwapp.doe.state.fl.us/EDW_Facts.htm.

Chapter 2

1. John S. Platt, Ann Cranston-Gingras, and John Scott Jr., "Understanding and Educating Migrant Students," *Preventing School Failure: Alternative Education for Children and Youth* 36, no. 1 (1991): 1–46.

2. Marni Finkelstein, Mark Wamsley, and Doreen Miranda, *What Keeps Children in Foster Care From Succeeding in School? Views of Early Adolescents and the Adults in Their Lives* (New York: Vera Institute of Justice, 2002).

3. Clifford Adelman, *Moving into Town—and Moving On: The Community College in the Lives of Traditional–age Students* (Washington, DC: U.S. Department of Education, 2005).

4. Lorin W. Anderson, Jacque Jacobs, Susan Schramm, and Fred Splittgerber, "School transitions: beginning of the end or a new beginning?" *International Journal of Educational Research* 33, no. 4 (2000): 325–39.

5. The term "community school" is also used to describe schools with an array of community resources for students and families available on-site, but these types of community schools are not considered to be part of the alternative education system and are not discussed here. Continuation schools, which offer more individualized instruction and smaller class sizes than large comprehensive high schools, are another form of alternative school not discussed here.

6. Elizabeth G. Hill, *Improving Alternative Education in California* (Sacramento, CA: Legislative Analyst's Office, 2007).

7. Jorge Ruiz de Velasco and Milbrey McLaughlin, *Raising the Bar, Building Capacity: Driving Improvement in California's Continuation High Schools* (Stanford and Berkeley, CA: John W. Gardner Center for Youth and Their Communities, Stanford University, and the Chief Justice Earl Warren Institute on Law and Social Policy, University of California, Berkeley, 2012).

8. William L. Carruthers, *Collected Evaluations on the WPCSS Alternative School Program for Students with Long-Term Suspensions* (Raleigh, NC: Wake County Public Schools Department of Evaluation and Research, 1999).

9. Katherine A.Magnuson, Marcia K. Meyers, Christopher J. Ruhm, and Jane Waldfogel, "Inequality in Preschool Education and School Readiness," *American Educational Research Journal* 41, no. 1 (2004):115–57.

10. Applied Survey Research, *School Readiness in San Mateo County: Results of the 2008 Assessment* (San Jose, CA: ASR, 2009).

11. W. Norton Grubb, Elizabeth Boner, Kate Frankel, Lynette Parker, David Patterson, Robert Gabriner, Laura Hope, Eva Schiorring, Bruce Smith, Richard Taylor, Ian Waltdon, and Smokey Wilson, *Understanding the "Crisis" in Basic Skills: Framing the Issues in Community Colleges* (Sacramento, CA: Policy Analysis for California Education, 2011).

12. James E. Rosenbaum, Regina Deil-Amen, and Ann E. Person, *After Admission: From College Access to College Success* (New York: Russell Sage Foundation, 2006).

13. Katherine L. Hughes and Judith Scott-Clayton, *Assessing Developmental Assessment in Community Colleges* (New York: Community College Resource Center, Teacher's College, Columbia University, 2011).

14. California Community College Student Success Task Force, *Advancing Student Success in the California Community Colleges: Recommendations of the California Community Colleges Student Success Task Force* (Sacramento, CA: California Community Colleges Chancellor's Office, 2012).

Chapter 3

1. Jacquelynne Eccles and Jennifer Gootman, *Community Programs to Promote Youth Development* (Washington, DC: National Academies Press, 2002).

2. Lynn M. Olson, Suk-fong S. Tang, and Paul W. Newacheck, "Children in the United States with Discontinuous Health Insurance Coverage," *New England Journal of Medicine* 353 (2005): 382–91.

3. Janet Currie, Sandra Decker, and Wanchuan Lin, "Has Public Health Insurance for Older Children Reduced Disparities in Access to Care and Health Outcomes?" *Journal of Health Economics* 27, no. 6 (2008):1567–81.

4. Rebecca A. London and Sebastian Castrechini, "Examining the Link Between Physical Fitness and Academic Achievement," *Journal of School Health* 81, no. 7 (2011): 400–08.

5. Rebecca A. London and Oded Gurantz, *Community-Based After School Programs and Youth Physical Fitness* (Stanford, CA: John W. Gardner Center for Youth and Their Communities, 2011).

Chapter 4

1. Milbrey W. McLaughlin, Merita A. Irby, and Juliet Langman, *Urban Sanctuaries: Neighborhood Organizations in the Lives and Futures of Inner-City Youth* (San Francisco: Jossey-Bass, 1994).

2. Marni Finkelstein, Mark Wamsley, and Doreen Miranda, *What Keeps Children in Foster Care from Succeeding in School? Views of Early Adolescents and the Adults in Their Lives* (New York: Vera Institute of Justice, 2002).

3. Thomas Parrish, John DuBois, Carolyn Delano, Donald Dixon, Daniel Webster, Jill Duerr Berrick, and Sally Bolus, *Education of Foster Group Home Children: Whose Responsibility Is It?* (Sacramento, CA: California Department of Education, 2001).

4. California Department of Education, *California Migrant Education Program: Comprehensive Needs Assessment* (Sacramento, CA: CDE, 2007).

5. John M. Bryson, Barbara C. Crosby, and Melissa Middleton Stone, "The Design and Implementation of Cross-Sector Collaborations: Propositions from the Literature," *Public Administration Review* 66, no. 1 (2006): 44–55.

6. In California, most schools are required to report average daily attendance (ADA) to receive state funding. ADA is calculated as the number of students in attendance on a certain day; if five students are absent on a given day in a school of one hundred students, that school's ADA is 95 percent for that day.

7. At the high school level, we are unable to separate all-day absences from partial-day absences for the 2006–07 through 2008–09 school years, therefore chronic absence rates cannot be calculated for these years.

8. Hedy N. Chang and Mariajosé Romero, *Present, Engaged, and Accounted For: The Critical Importance of Addressing Chronic Absence in the Early Grades* (New York: National Center for Children in Poverty, 2008).

9. Mariajosé Romero and Young-Sun Lee, *A National Portrait of Chronic Absenteeism in the Early Grades* (New York: National Center for Children in Poverty, 2007).

Chapter 5

1. Ruby, a City College student, was interviewed several times as part of a case study project carried out by Laurie Scolari. Scolari came to know Ruby when she served as a Student Ambassador, a program Scolari oversees. "Ruby" is a pseudonym.

2. National Student Clearinghouse data allow high schools to track the postsecondary enrollment and success of their graduates at most public and private institutions in the United States but does not provide detailed information such as students' course transcripts.

3. The English CST is a component of state accountability models, but is not used for determining high school graduation or college eligibility.

Chapter 6

1. Carla M. Roach and Milbrey McLaughlin, *The Redwood City 2020 Collaborative: Building Capacity for Community Youth Development* (Stanford, CA: John W. Gardner Center for Youth and Their Communities, 2008).

2. Sebastian Castrechini, *Examining Student Outcomes Across Programs in Redwood City Community Schools* (Stanford, CA: John W. Gardner Center for Youth and Their Communities, 2011).

3. Roach and McLaughlin, *Redwood City 2020 Collaborative.*

Chapter 7

1. Chapter 6 provides detail on the Redwood City 2020 collaborative.

2. Richard M. Ryan and Edward L. Deci, "Self-Determination Theory and the Facilitation of Intrinsic Motivation, Social Development, and Well-being," *American Psychologist* 55, no. 1 (2000): 68–78.

3. Martin J. Blank and Amy Berg, *All Together Now: Sharing Responsibility for the Whole Child* (Washington, DC: Association for Supervision and Curriculum Development, 2006).

Chapter 8

1. Sandra Nutley, Isabel Walter, and Huw T. O. Davies, "Promoting Evidence-based Practice: Models and Mechanisms from Cross-Sector Review," *Research on Social Work Practice* 19, no. 5 (2009): 552–59.

2. Julie A. Marsh, John F. Pane, and Laura S. Hamilton, *Making Sense of Data-Driven Decision Making in Education*, Rand Education Occasional Paper, 2006, http://www.rand.org/pubs/occasional_papers/2006/RAND_OP170.pdf.

3. Nutley et al., "Promoting Evidence-based Practice," 552–59.

4. Department of Education, Training, and Youth Affairs, "The Impact of Educational Research—an Overview," in *The Impact of Educational Research: Research Evaluation Programme* (Canberra: DETYA, 2000), 3–13.

5. Jane Hemsley-Brown and Caroline Sharp, "The Use of Research to Improve Professional Practice: A Systematic Review of the Literature," *Oxford Review of Education* 29, no. 4 (2003): 449–71.

6. Vivian Tseng, "The Uses of Research in Policy and Practice," *Social Policy Report* 26, no. 2 (2012): 1–16.

7. Anita M. Zervigon-Hakes, "Translating Research Findings into Large-Scale Public Programs and Policy," *The Future of Children* 5, no. 3 (1995): 175–91.

8. Dennis P. Culhane, John Fantuzzo, Heather L. Rouse, Vicky Tam, and Jonathan Lukens, "Connecting the Dots: The Promise of Integrated Data Systems for Policy Analysis and Systems Reform," *Intelligence for Social Policy* (2010): 1–22, http://works.bepress.com/dennis_culhane/90/.

9. Melissa Jonson-Reid and Brett Drake, "Multisector Longitudinal Administrative Databases: An Indispensable Tool for Evidence-Based Policy for Maltreated Children and Their Families," *Child Maltreatment* 13, no. 4 (2008): 392–99.

10. Ibid.

11. Marsh et al., *Making Sense.*

12. DETYA, *Impact of Educational Research.*

13. Marsh et al., *Making Sense.*

14. Tseng, "Uses of Research," 1–16.

15. Culhane et al., "Connecting the Dots," 1–22.

16. Susan Smith, Deborah Staub, Mary Myslewicz, and Elizabeth Laird, *Linking Education and Social Service Data to Improve Child Welfare,* Casey Family Programs and Data Quality Campaign, 2007, http://www.DataQualityCampaign.org/

17. Rebecca Carson, Elizabeth Laird, Elizabeth Gaines, and Thaddeus Ferber, *Linking Data Across Agencies: States That Are Making It Work* (2009 draft), Data Quality Campaign and Forum for Youth Investment, http://www.DataQualityCampaign.org/

18. Ingrid Nelson, Karen Strobel, and Rebecca London, "Making Sausage: Multi-Level Relationship Building in University-School Research Collaborations" (paper presented at the American Educational Research Association Annual Meeting, Denver, CO, May 2010).

19. Zervigon-Hakes, "Translating Research Programs," 175–91.

20. Milbrey W. McLaughlin, W. Richard Scott, Sarah N. Deschenes, Kathryn C. Hopkins, and Anne R. Newman, *Between Movement and Establishment: Organizations Advocating for Youth* (Stanford, CA: Stanford University Press, 2009).

Appendix 1

1. "Overview of the Privacy Act of 1974," U.S. Department of Justice, http://www.justice.gov/opcl/1974privacyact-overview.htm.

2. Ibid.

3. Family Educational Rights and Privacy Act (FERPA), 20 U.S.C. § 1232g (1974).

4. "Educational records" in this case are 1) directly related to the student, and 2) maintained by an educational agency or institution or by a party acting for the agency or institution.

5. "Family Educational Rights and Privacy; Final Rule," U.S. Department of Education, http://www.gpo.gov/fdsys/pkg/FR-2011-12-02/html/2011-30683.htm.

6. "Summary of the HIPAA Privacy Rule," U.S. Department of Health and Human Services, http://www.hhs.gov/ocr/privacy/hipaa/understanding/ summary/index.html.

7. "California Civil Code Section 1798.24-1798.24b," State of California, http://www.leginfo.ca.gov/cgi-bin/displaycode?section=civ&group=01001-02000&file=1798.24-1798.24b.

8. "California Education Code Section 49073-49079.7," California Department of Education, http://www.leginfo.ca.gov/cgi-bin/displaycode?section=edc&group=49001-50000&file=49073-49079.7.

9. "California Education Code Section 49073-49079.7."

10. "California Welfare and Institutions Code Section 10850-10853," California Department of Social Services, http://www.leginfo.ca.gov/cgi-bin/displaycode?section=wic&group=10001-11000&file=10850-10853.

11. "Manual of Policies and Procedures: Confidentiality, Fraud, Civil Rights, and State Hearings," California Department of Social Services, http://www.cdss.ca.gov/cdssweb/entres/getinfo/pdf/1cfcman.pdf.

ACKNOWLEDGMENTS

This book represents the efforts not only of the authors and editors but also of many other Youth Data Archive researchers and partners who contributed substantially to the approach and research. Peggy O'Brien-Strain worked on the initial YDA concept of empowering local communities to harness their own data for cross-sector work; she brought critical skills and policy experience to the Archive's design and development and provided a first home for its data. Former John W. Gardner Center staff members Jon Norman and Nora Mallonee and graduate research assistant Betsy Williams played key roles in contributing to YDA analyses and building strong relationships with community partners. Other current and former Gardner Center staff provided critical support to the book-writing process, including Larissa Collins, Carmen Rodriguez, Angela Ongoco, Nina Duong, and Leslie Patron.

None of this work would be possible, of course, without the commitment and support of our community partners. We especially thank our Redwood City partners for their belief in the YDA concept before it was a reality. Ed Everett, then City Manager, provided enthusiastic backing for the concept and the new Stanford relationship it represented. Pat Brown, Executive Director of Redwood City 2020, has been from the outset an especially important collaborator for this work, ensuring open communication channels and leaders' buy-in.

Many of the partners referenced throughout the book have contributed not only data to the YDA, but also funding to support specific analyses. The YDA initiative has also been supported by a variety of other funders and we thank the Atlantic Philanthropies, the Center for American Progress, the Evelyn and Walter Haas Jr. Fund, the William and Flora Hewlett

Foundation, the James Irvine Foundation, the Robert Wood Johnson Foundation, the Rosenberg Foundation, the Ewing Marion Kauffman Foundation, the David and Lucile Packard Foundation, the Skoll Foundation, the Spencer Foundation, the Thrive Foundation for Youth, and the Walton Family Foundation for their belief and investment in this work.

Finally, we thank the editorial staff at Harvard Education Press for their support of this project.

ABOUT THE EDITORS

Milbrey McLaughlin, EdD, is the David Jacks Professor of Education and Public Policy, Emerita, at Stanford University and the founding director of the John W. Gardner Center for Youth and Communities. She also is codirector of the Center for Research on the Context of Teaching, an interdisciplinary research center engaged in analyses of how teaching and learning are shaped by teachers' organizational, institutional, and social-cultural contexts. McLaughlin has focused throughout her career on the various institutional contexts and policies that shape youth outcomes—schools and community-based institutions most particularly. The JGC embodies McLaughlin's interest in identifying and understanding the cross-institutional issues that shape the settings within and through which youth move, and in advancing a "youth sector" stance to inform policy and practice. She is the author or coauthor of many books, articles, and chapters on education policy issues, contexts for teaching and learning, productive environments for youth, and communitybased organizations. Her recent books include: *Between Movement and Establishment: Organizations Advocating for Youth,* Stanford University Press, 2009; *Building School-based Teacher Learning Communities,* Teachers College Press, 2006; *School Districts and Instructional Renewal,* Teachers College Press, 2002; and *Communities of Practice and the Work of High School Teaching,* University of Chicago Press, 2001. Dr. McLaughlin holds an EdM and EdD in education policy from the Harvard Graduate School of Education and a BA in philosophy from Connecticut College.

Rebecca A. London, PhD, is Senior Researcher at the John W. Gardner Center for Youth and Communities and the researcher overseeing all analyses conducted with the Youth Data Archive. She has been with the Center since 2005. Throughout her career, London's research has bridged academia and policy, focusing on the policies and programs intended to serve low-income or disadvantaged families and youth. Using both qualitative and quantitative methods, London has conducted research on a variety of policy-relevant topics such as physical fitness and academic achievement, secondary to postsecondary transitions, the effects of after-school program participation, the digital divide for youth, the effects of welfare reform, college attendance among low-income mothers, and children's living arrangements. Her work has been published in journals such as the *Journal of Policy Analysis and Management, Social Science Quarterly, the Journal of Higher Education, Journal of School Health, Journal of Education for Students Placed at Risk,* and *Youth & Society.* She has also written many reports and briefs aimed at a nonacademic policy and practitioner audience. Dr. London holds a PhD in human development and social policy from Northwestern University's School of Education and Social Policy, an MA in economics, also from Northwestern, and a BA in economics from the University of Michigan.

ABOUT THE CONTRIBUTORS

Maureen Carew leads the postsecondary success programs for San Francisco Unified School District, including Bridge to Success and SF Promise—system change initiatives working with City College of San Francisco, San Francisco State, and the San Francisco Mayor's Office. Through these initiatives, policy and practice changes at these institutions have come to be driven by data analysis. Prior to working for the school district Carew served as executive director of several San Francisco nonprofits serving low-income or disadvantaged families and youth. Carew specializes in public-private collaborations leveraging community-based assets to increase efficacy of public institutions serving families. She served as a Peace Corps volunteer in Paraguay. Ms. Carew is a first-generation college graduate and received her BA from Franklin Pierce College.

Sebastian Castrechini, EdM, is a senior policy analyst at the John W. Gardner Center for Youth and Their Communities at Stanford University, working primarily with the Youth Data Archive. Castrechini has been at the JGC for over four years and previously worked as both a school teacher and administrator. Castrechini's areas of research expertise include community schools and youth fitness and wellness. He has published quantitative and GIS-based research in the _Journal of School Health_ and _Penn GSE Perspectives on Urban Education_, and has presented at the National Institutes of Health, American Educational Research Association, and Coalition for Community Schools conferences. Mr. Castrechini holds a BS in secondary education in social studies from Penn State University and a Master's of Education in education policy from the Harvard Graduate School of Education.

Jan Christensen joined the Redwood City School District as superintendent in May 2006. Under Christensen's leadership, the Redwood City School District embraced new instructional strategies and an emphasis on data-driven instruction that has resulted in significant academic gains and a narrowing of the achievement gap among its diverse student population. Christensen has been an active member of the Redwood City community, serving as president of the San Mateo County Superintendent's Association, vice chair of the San Mateo County of Education SELPA Board, vice chair of the Redwood City Chamber of Commerce, and on the Sequoia Hospital Community Advisory Council. Christensen was born and raised outside of Detroit, Michigan. She began her work in education in 1978 in Plymouth, Michigan, as a middle school teacher, teaching grades 6–8. In 1981 she moved to Alaska and taught at Sitka High School for one year and Clark Middle School for five years. Following a one-year internship, Christensen served as an Anchorage assistant principal for two years, first at Hanshew Middle School and then at Mears Middle School. She served as an assistant principal at East High School for three years before being appointed as principal at Chugiak High School. From July 2001 to April 2006 Christensen was the Anchorage School District's assistant superintendent for curriculum and instruction. Ms. Christensen graduated from Eastern Michigan University, where she earned a BA in history and minored in English. She also earned an MA from Eastern Michigan University in educational leadership. She has completed post-masters coursework in leadership, curriculum, and instruction at Gonzaga University in their doctoral program. She has also been an adjunct professor at the University of Alaska, Anchorage, where she taught courses in curriculum and leadership, organizational development and leadership, and politics and education.

Kara Dukakis, LCSW, is the associate director of the John W. Gardner Center for Youth and Communities. She has been at the Center for close to five years, focusing on the strategic direction of the organization and overseeing the community engagement and research translation of Youth Data Archive analyses. A licensed clinical social worker by training, Dukakis has spent the past fifteen years developing policy, bridging policy and practice, and translating research in the areas of child welfare, child and family mental health, and early childhood education, the latter with a specific emphasis on postsecondary education among early childhood providers. She has written a number of reports on universal preschool and early childhood education policy and was appointed by the San Francisco Board of Supervisors to a four-year term on the San Francisco First Five Children and Families Commission, two of which she served as chair. Ms. Dukakis holds an MA in social welfare from the University of California, Berkeley, and a BA in political science from Brown University.

Amy Gerstein, PhD, has served as executive director of the John W. Gardner Center for Youth and Their Communities at Stanford University since August 2009. Amy is responsible for the overall strategic direction of the Center while engaging in research and community partnership work directly. She sits on the board of the East Palo Alto YMCA. Gerstein's research and strategic work has focused primarily on policy, district reform, leadership development, professional development, organizational development, evaluation, and instructional improvement. Prior to the JGC, Gerstein was an education research and policy consultant providing services to foundations, educational organizations, and other nonprofits. She has also served as the executive director of the Noyce Foundation in Palo Alto, California. Prior to that, Gerstein served as the executive director of the Coalition of Essential Schools, an international school reform network. Previous to this position, she was the associate director of the Bay Area School Reform Collaborative in San Francisco. She has also taught high school science, outdoor education, and teacher education. Dr. Gerstein holds a PhD in education from Stanford University and a BA in geology-biology from Brown University.

Oded Gurantz joined the John W. Gardner Center for Youth and Their Communities in 2006 and is a senior policy analyst for the Youth Data Archive initiative. His recent work focuses on linking longitudinal data across public agencies to explore student pathways through the K–16 system, with a strong focus on the transition from secondary to postsecondary education. Prior to his graduate studies, Gurantz worked for Project SEED, teaching mathematics to elementary school students in Oakland, California, and at the Escuela Mayatan in Copan Ruinas, Honduras. Mr. Gurantz received an MS in applied economics and finance from the University of California, Santa Cruz, and a BA in mathematics from the University of California, Berkeley.

Monika Sanchez is a policy analyst at the John W. Gardner Center for Youth and Their Communities at Stanford University. Sanchez works primarily with the Gardner Center's Youth Data Archive initiative and has extensive experience working with data for public policy and planning purposes. Her research expertise includes the connection between preschool participation and elementary outcomes, the causes and consequences of student absenteeism, and student health and wellness. She has presented at the American Educational Research Association, Applied Demography, and Population Association of America conferences. Ms. Sanchez holds an MS in population and development from the London School of Economics and Political Science and a BA in economics from the University of California, San Diego.

Laurie Scolari, EdD, has worked toward accomplishing her goal of increasing the number of first-generation college students who complete a certificate or degree in institutions of higher education for over seventeen years. Her areas of expertise include policy reform within institutions of higher education, K–12/university partnerships, and multimillion dollar grant management. She is currently the dean of counseling and student support services and has also served as the associate dean of outreach and recruitment services at City College of San Francisco. In that capacity, she spearheaded several successful data-driven initiatives aimed at minimizing the local achievement gap with sustainable results. Previously, Scolari served as the Early Academic Outreach Program (EAOP) director, Gaining Early Awareness for Undergraduate Program (GEAR UP) director, and associate director of the Educational Partnership Center at the University of California, Santa Cruz. Dr. Scolari holds a doctorate in educational leadership from San Francisco State University, an MA in nonprofit administration from the University of San Francisco, and a BA in communications from San Jose State University.

Karen R. Strobel, PhD, is a senior research associate at the John W. Gardner Center for Youth and Their Communities working on the Middle School Survey. She has been with the Center for nearly ten years. Her research focuses on adolescent development in school and out-of-school settings, achievement motivation, and low-income community contexts. Drawing on her expertise in social-cognitive models of motivation, she studies successful developmental pathways among low-income early adolescents. Her work has been published in journals such as the *Teachers College Record, Journal of Adolescent Research*, and *American Behavioral Scientist*. Dr. Strobel holds a PhD in education from Stanford University with a concentration in child and adolescent development.

Lisa Westrich, LCSW, joined the John W. Gardner Center for Youth and Their Communities in 2009 as a research and policy analyst. Westrich is a qualitative researcher whose recent work focuses on family engagement practices in community schools, community youth development, and student health and wellness in low-income schools. She is a licensed clinical social worker with expertise in adolescent development and mental health. Westrich has held various nonprofit leadership positions and has worked directly with youth and families in a variety of education and community settings for the last twenty years. She also has experience in school and clinic-based research and in program development and implementation, and she has provided clinical consultation to a number of local nonprofits. Ms. Westrich holds an MS in social work from Columbia University and a BA in mass communications from the University of California, Berkeley.

INDEX